Ian Frazier is the author of *Great Plains, On the Rez,* and *Dating Your Mom,* among other works, all published by Farrar, Straus and Giroux. A frequent contributor to *The New Yorker,* he lives in Montclair, New Jersey.

ALSO BY IAN FRAZIER

Dating Your Mom

Nobody Better, Better Than Nobody

Great Plains

Family

Coyote v. Acme

On the Rez

It Happened Like This (translator)

The Fish's Eye

GONE TO NEW YORK

GONE TO NEW YORK

ADVENTURES IN THE CITY

IAN FRAZIER

Picador
Farrar, Straus and Giroux
New York

www.picadorusa.com

Picador® is a U.S. registered trademark and is used by Farrar, Straus and Giroux
under license from Pan Books Limited.

For information on Picador Reading Group Guides,
as well as ordering, please contact Picador.
Phone: 646-307-5629
Fax: 212-253-9627
E-mail: readinggroupguides@picadorusa.com

Grateful acknowledgment is made to *The Atlantic Monthly,*
DoubleTake, Mother Jones, New York, and *The New Yorker,*
where these pieces first appeared, in slightly different form.

Design by Jonathan D. Lippincott

ISBN-13: 978-0-312-42504-3
ISBN-10: 0-321-42504-X

First published in the United States by Farrar, Straus and Giroux

D 10 9 8 7 6 5

To Jamaica Kincaid

CONTENTS

CONTENTS

FOREWORD

BY JAMAICA KINCAID

To write an introduction to a collection of essays written by my dearest friend in all the still sphere-shaped world, I have to write about our youth and what he was like when I first met him, as he was just arriving in New York and hired by *The New Yorker* as a Talk writer.

In the spring of 1973, I met Sandy outside a movie theater on Eighth Avenue where the movie *Thomasine & Bushrod* was being shown for the first time to a general audience. George W. S. Trow, then an established writer for *The New Yorker*, introduced us. George was the most fascinating person we had ever met. He knew all sorts of wonderful things about New York and all sorts of people, some of whom were not so wonderful. We, Sandy and I, became George's younger siblings almost immediately. He thought we were pretty smart but ignorant, and he was always doing his best to educate and civilize us. He introduced me to Jacqueline Onassis and he introduced Sandy to Mrs. Vreeland. We didn't like either of them. He made us read Proust. Sandy read all six volumes, I stopped where I always stop: at volume three. He took Sandy to a store that sold good-quality men's clothing and bought him a beige poplin summer suit. Once, when Sandy was feeling gloomy, George jokingly asked him if he wanted to go to Payne Whitney and have a soothing entrée. Sandy, thinking Payne Whitney was a restaurant, said yes. George said, "Oh dear." George started an anti-rudeness campaign that came to an end when one day, on the subway, after he corrected someone's behavior, he got punched in the eye.

That afternoon outside the theater showing *Thomasine & Bushrod* where I first met Sandy, he was wearing a coat made of green cloth. The coat looked like something a spy would wear, an American spy, or something a soldier would wear, an American soldier. He wore the coat all the time. To him it symbolized, and that is the correct word, his Ohio-ness. Oh, Ohio, Ohio, Ohio. That's all we ever heard about, that's all he ever talked about. Now, the state of Ohio occupies a very large area, and I did know that at the time, but in those first years when I knew Sandy Frazier, not Ian Frazier but Sandy Frazier, I came to really believe that Ohio was made up of a little bit of some unnameable area; Cleveland, which was bigger but not by too much than the unnameable area; and then, overwhelmingly, Hudson, the place where Sandy was born and spent his childhood and left when he went East to Harvard and which he returned to often when he was a young writer at *The New Yorker*.

I soon came to believe that anything claiming to be authentically American originated from Ohio and, in particular, Hudson, Ohio. The Rosenthals, parents of Sandy's girlfriend, Suzy. The Bartlows, parents of his best friend

Ken. The Erskines, parents of his best friend Don. Particularly authentic were Mrs. Erskine's garden tips, which consisted mainly of getting Don and Sandy to weed her garden, and Mrs. Erskine listening to the opera broadcast on the radio every Saturday afternoon. His household cat, which he would terrify by crawling around the floor on his hands and knees while dressed in his mother's fur coat. His family's housekeeper, whom he insulted because he suspected she liked his brother best. (She did.) His parents were the most authentic parents in America, especially his mother, whom he adored and who adored him. But when he wrote a piece called "Dating Your Mom," a way of enshrining his adoration, while at the same time making fun of it, she was not pleased; he could tell, for she never mentioned it, she acted as if it had never happened. I loved his authentic family, made up of a brother, two sisters, and his mother and father. I loved them before I met them, particularly his mother. And my love for her turned out to be completely justified.

After she died and Sandy was going through her papers, he found a folder in which she kept everything I had published. Hard as he looked, he could find no such folder containing his own writing. To understand why this made us both laugh, it's important to know that he suffers from a serious case of sibling rivalry. From the earliest days of knowing Sandy, he has been my true, true brother, the only brother I have ever needed.

This authentic America that Sandy knew intimately because it emanated from Hudson, Ohio, because without Hudson, Ohio, authentic America could not exist, did not include the Southern states, the slave states. His father, David Frazier, once put some very close relatives (an aunt and uncle who were visiting from Alabama) out of his house because they used a derogatory word for African-Americans in conversation in the living room. Once, George said there had been some good things about the institution of slavery as practiced in the American South before 1864 and this made Sandy so mad he walked all the way from midtown Manhattan up to the George Washington Bridge and hitch-hiked to Hudson, Ohio.

The authentic America that Sandy knew (then) and knows (now) begins with Abraham Lincoln (excepting some small unpleasantness with the original Americans) and the right side of the Civil War and the Emancipation and Lewis and Clark, whom he extracts from an earlier time and places in a more beautifully just America, and also Crazy Horse and Sitting Bull and the vast, vast, vast openness of the West with its ancient history of unsettledness, settledness, and un-settledness again; and also fishing, fly-fishing to be exact; en-counters with bears; an examination of life on a Rte., a major transportation artery, from which it is possible to re-turn to Hudson, Ohio. The authentic America includes his immediate ancestors, Protestants all, seeking refuge in vari-ous American Christian sects as they tried to save themselves from their own certainties. How my dear friend and brother loves this act, a person, an individual, trying to save himself from their own convictions.

My friend Sandy's father was such a person. He was a chemist and worked for Standard Oil of Ohio, trying to make various forms of plastics from petroleum. He loved making plastics from petroleum. That was during the day. At night he read *The New Yorker* to his son, especially the writings of E. B. White. It was his father reading to him from *The New Yorker* that made Sandy want to leave Hudson, Ohio, and go to New York and become a writer. After he left Harvard, he applied for a job at *The New Yorker*. They offered him a job as a checker, that is, a person who would check the facts as they appeared in other writers' writing. Sandy refused it. *The New Yorker* then was a magical place: in whatever position you entered it, you were doomed to stay there. So if you entered *The New Yorker* as a checker, or as a writer, or as an editor, you were doomed to that role only. It was like life itself: no matter who you are in life, you are doomed to life itself. Not long after he rejected the position of checker, *The New Yorker* offered him a job as a Talk writer. It was right around then we met.

Sandy wore the green coat all the time. Other people wore clothes that were completely different. It was the disco era or sometime near it. No one we knew in New York did anything remotely serious, except for George's friend whose father had once been the mayor of New York, and there were some other people whom George knew who did serious things, or so George said, for he was always telling Sandy and me about the other serious people he knew. Many of the other people George knew we thought should be shot, though not shot dead, just shot in a Bugs Bunny sort of way, where they get up again. Sandy and I hated serious people. The exception was Mr. Shawn, the editor of *The New Yorker*. He was the only serious person we loved, and even better, he was the only serious person we took seriously. We took him so seriously that we often brushed him off. From time to time, Mr. Shawn would suggest ideas for Talk stories to Sandy and every time Sandy would say to him that his suggestions were terrible. Sandy would just say outright, over the telephone, in a note, or face-to-face with Mr. Shawn, that his idea was terrible. Mr. Shawn's ideas weren't terrible at all. How could they be? But we, Sandy and I, had decided, for reasons that we could not then articulate, never to agree to Mr. Shawn's suggestions. My own reasons for doing so are clear to me. Sandy's reasons for doing so reside for me with those obstructionist Protestants that he comes from and whom he has written about (see his book *Family*). How he liked defying then. He had convictions, I didn't know exactly what they were, but he felt compelled to save himself from them.

But that green cloth coat again, which made Sandy seem as if he were a spy or a lost agent of our government: it was an army surplus item. Sandy wore it and wore it, no matter what the season. One day, while he was wearing it, he came into my office at *The New Yorker* and said he had agreed to join the army or the navy or maybe it was the marines, I can't remember now, except that when he told me this, I said to him, Oh Sandy, you can't do that, you're too old. He said then, Yeah, you're right. It was quite complicated then to de-enlist but I didn't know that and he only told this to me not too long ago. There was a moment where we (George Trow and I, for the three of us were sometimes inseparable) thought he was a stranger from somewhere else. I came from Antigua, a small island in the West Indies, and George came from Connecticut, a small area of the original

American enterprise, and dear Sandy from Hudson, Ohio, was a shock. It was because Sandy, while wearing the green cloth coat, which was authentically American (it too came from Hudson, Ohio), became sad that George suggested to him the possibility of the soothing entrée at the Payne Whitney psychiatric hospital, but at that time, because Sandy was authentically American, he was not so familiar with Payne Whitney and psychiatric hospitals.

The green cloth coat came to an end in this way: From time to time, as a joke and out of the blue, Sandy would say to George, "George, do you want a steak?" and George would say "Yes." This was a set piece. After a long set of back and forth humiliating one-upsmanship jokes between the two of them, Sandy would ask George if he wanted a steak and George would always answer that he did. One day, after George said yes, Sandy went down to the Jefferson Market, a fancy grocery store even then, and bought a very expensive steak, placed it unwrapped in the pocket of his green cloth coat, and presented it to George. That time, when he asked George, Do you want a steak? and George said yes, he took a piece of raw prime beef out of his green coat pocket and gave it to him. This all took place in George's office, an office he shared with Tony Hiss. I remember it because George, who was shocked by the actual appearance of the steak, did a good job of not showing how impressed he was by this whole brief gesture with its long preceding narrative; and I remember it because George gave me the steak and I took it to my little apartment which I rented on West Twenty-second Street, and cooked it according to a recipe in *Mastering the Art of French Cooking*. The steak made such a mess in the pocket of Sandy's green coat, he couldn't wear it anymore. I cannot remember what replaced it.

The authentic American hated English people. So did I. George wasn't an Anglophile, it was just that he liked aristocrats. The two of us now formed a camp: we couldn't understand how George liked Mrs. Vreeland, yet we loved George because he knew Mrs. Vreeland and a great many other people like her whom I personally wanted to place on a bonfire, but only if no one, no one on the face of the earth, could observe me. One day, when I was trying to read a biography of Lytton Strachey, written by another Englishman, Sandy was so outraged that instead of laughing at his antics I preferred to read this book, he tore it out of my hand and proceeded to read it himself. From this came a piece, a parody, a *New Yorker* casual titled "The Bloomsbury Group, Live at the Apollo." In this short, funny piece of writing, Sandy reduced two people who are a substantial part of modern consciousness, however you look at it (Virginia Woolf and Maynard Keynes), to desperate performers at the Apollo Theater, a venue for many black modern artists who were so beyond their time that there would never be a time for them. At that time in *The New Yorker*'s life, S. J. Perelman appeared in the magazine. Funny people wrote funny things and these funny things spilled over into the realm of literature. Yet when I saw that piece, knowing its origins as well as I did, I asked myself, How did he do that? And that thought has never stopped occurring to me; to this day, when I read something new that he has written, I think, How did he do that?

FOREWORD

The collection begins with a couple of Talk pieces and ends with his memory of great Hudson, Ohio. But this end is really the beginning. It is from Hudson that he ventures forth into the wild lands of lower Manhattan, to live for a time or just to find a typewriter; to Brooklyn; to Queens; to invent a tool that will remove plastic bags from trees (his father did work in plastics), a tool so expensive that if he had not invented it he would not be able to own one. It is such a pleasure to read this collection of my dearest friend's work, and to see that it is meant to form an arc, an arc that has not yet begun its curve.

GONE TO NEW YORK

ANTIPODES

If you drilled a hole straight through the earth, starting at the corner of Seventh Avenue and Forty-second Street, you would pass through ten inches of pavement, four feet of pipes, thirty-five feet of Seventh Avenue subway, about twenty-two hundred miles of rock, about thirty-six hundred miles of nickel-iron core, and then another twenty-two hundred miles of rock. You would come out in the Indian Ocean, 106°3' east longitude and 40°45' south latitude, about three hundred miles off the southwest coast of Australia. You would have reached Manhattan's antipodes, or diametrically opposite point on the globe. You would be about two and a half miles under water.

Due north of Manhattan's antipodes, it is 2,040 miles to Malingping, Java. Due south, it is 1,500 miles to the Knox Coast of Antarctica, 2,260 miles to the Russian research station at Vostok, Antarctica, and 2,955 miles to the South Pole. Due west, it is 7,700 miles to Punta Rasa (Flat Point), Argentina. Due east, it is 1,760 miles to Cape Grim, Tasmania. The town nearest to Manhattan's antipodes is Augusta,

Australia, 590 miles to the northeast, where Australians go for fishing vacations and where it rains about half the year.

Not much goes on in this part of the Indian Ocean. It is fall there now. The water is gray-green, like the North Atlantic, and very rough. Navigators call these latitudes "the roaring forties," because the storms are so violent. There are no shipping lanes near Manhattan's antipodes, so there is no junk on the ocean floor. The ocean floor is completely dark (except for the light produced by occasional luminescent fish and other organisms), and the water at the bottom is only a few degrees above freezing. A white, squishy substance known as globigerina ooze covers the ocean floor. Glob ooze, as oceanographers call it, is a calcium sediment made of the shells of globigerina, which are tiny foraminiferal organisms. Glob ooze can be anywhere from less than an inch to a thousand feet thick. Since it is too much trouble to wash the salt out of it even to make cement, glob ooze has no commercial value. This far from land, there are few fish. A school of whales might pass by seasonally. There might be a few rattails (bottom-feeders related to the shark family) near the ocean floor.

If you could walk northeast to Australia, wearing some kind of glob-ooze shoes to keep from sinking in, as well as equipment to deal with the problems of air, light, temperature, and water pressure, you would have to cross underwater mountains of sixty-four hundred feet and descend nineteen thousand feet into valleys before you ascended Australia's continental slope, nearly four hundred miles away. Manhattan's antipodes lies on the southeastern branch of the Mid-Indian Oceanic Ridge, which is a Y-shaped ridge in the middle of the Indian Ocean with heights of ten thousand feet and valleys as deep as fourteen thousand feet. The Mid-Oceanic Ridge is the longest continuous feature on the earth's surface. Dr. Bruce Heezen, of Columbia's Lamont-Doherty Geological Observatory (one of the few New Yorkers who have ever been close to Manhattan's antipodes), made the first detailed map of the Indian Ocean floor, under the auspices of the International Indian Ocean Expedition, in the early 1960s. He says that the discovery and exploration of the Mid-Oceanic Ridge provided the conclusive proof for the theory of continental drift. "About fifty million years ago, the ridge moved through Antarctica and chipped off a huge piece—Australia—which then headed north and rotated slightly counterclockwise until it crashed into Indonesia," he said. "It did not take long, in geological time. When we discovered that ridge, and when we found that the central and eastern Indian Ocean was much younger than the western Indian Ocean, the theory of continental drift was finally accepted. Before this discovery, if you believed in drift you couldn't get a job. Now if you don't you can't."

About the biggest thing that has ever happened near Manhattan's antipodes happened three hundred miles away, in the course of the International Indian Ocean Expedition. A British member of Parliament, on board the Australian ship *Diamantina*, was mapping the ocean floor with an echo sounder that was faulty—something he did not realize. About three hundred miles southwest of Australia, he and his shipmates started getting some extremely deep soundings. They became very excited about this and later claimed to the press that they had found the deepest point in the oceans. They named their find the Diamantina Trench. When their claim was investigated, it turned out to be wrong. The Diamantina Trench, even at its deepest point, is only about twenty-two thousand feet deep, which is considerably shallower than the deepest ocean trenches.

Two of our favorite Midwestern towns—Pekin, Illinois, and Canton, Illinois—were so named because their founders thought that the towns were exactly opposite the two famous Chinese cities. Pekin, Ill., and Canton, Ill., are in fact opposite points in the Indian Ocean some seven hundred miles to the west of New York's opposite point. Most of the United States is opposite the southern Indian Ocean. There is no point in the United States where, if you drilled straight through the earth, you would come out in China.

(1975)

RENTAL

The southwest windows of my third-floor loft face on one of the most harum-scarum intersections in the city, where Sixth Avenue, Varick Street (Seventh Avenue), West Broadway, and Thompson Street, pinched by the narrowness of Manhattan, dump huge loads of traffic into the already rich mixture of cars and trucks heading east and west on Canal Street between the Manhattan Bridge and the Holland Tunnel. The intersection is really more of an open-air car mall, where stoplights function in a largely advisory capacity, where "WALK" signs are jokes, and where car horns are heard just about nonstop during rush hours and the Feast of San Gennaro. Car horns, and occasional truck horns that lift me clean out of bed on summer nights when I have the windows open, and screeching tires, and the violent hiss of air brakes, and, about twice a year, collisions (last year a guy trying the highly prized and difficult post-green-light turn from Canal onto West Broadway smashed into the window of the luncheonette on the corner; nobody hurt)—these are mainly what I hear in my apartment. The only human sounds that come through it all are arguments between drivers, and the word "Fireworks," which Italian and Chinese kids shout to passing cars during the week before the Fourth of July. Even at this time of year, I spend a lot of time on my fire escape looking at the cars—I have about a 90 percent accuracy in picking cars from New Jersey—and in the summer I love to watch rain come into the intersection. When rain comes from the west, the sky is often a translucent green, like the glass in a doctor's office door, and the large raindrops hit so hard that you can see the smaller drops that fly off in a circle from the impact, and the cars' windshield wipers switch to superfast with a nerve-racking sound. When rain comes from the east in a very dark thunderhead—something that happens more rarely—you can see the brightness-activated streetlights all the way along Canal pop on one at a time under the advancing storm.

I went out on my fire escape last Friday morning to take my first look at the largest object I had ever rented: a six-yard rubbish container from Timothy Duffy Rubbish Removal. My loft (it used to be one floor of a candy company) had at that time a lot of rubbish in it. Old doors, cork insulation, busted stepladders, lumber, pieces of pipe—things that were too large to fall under the heading of either trash or garbage, and that the regular trash guys would not take if I left them on the street. For a while, I tried just putting rubbish on the street and hoping to forget about it, but the trash men would leave it for days in protest, and people would go through it. I cannot stand people going through my rubbish. Once, a friend of mine, after many years of owning a red quilt with her initials on it that her mother had made, threw it out, only to see a woman wearing it a few days later near Gramercy Park. This is the kind of thing I fear. So first I called another rubbish-removal firm, and they said that they would send somebody around to look at my rubbish and give me an estimate—exactly what I was trying to avoid. Then I talked to my landlord, and his thoughts turned to bribery; he suggested that I take the rubbish out a day at a time and stay up until three in the morning, when the regular trash men come, and give them some money. Neither of those ideas appealing to me, I went over to Duffy and ordered, sight unseen, its smallest container, a six-yarder, for sixty-five dollars.

Before I saw it, I thought that a six-yard container would be six yards long, and I was afraid that I would not have enough rubbish to fill it and would end up throwing away stuff that I actually wanted to keep—my TV, chest of drawers, and stereo—in order not to appear ridiculous in the eyes of my landlord, his brother, and his friends. ("Look at that idiot. He pays sixty-five dollars for a railroad car to put a couple Hefty bags in. What an idiot.") However, after one look at the container I realized that six yards was a cubic measurement, and that this container and my volume of rubbish were made for each other. As my friend Andy and I carried out junk through the morning, I found the container a comforting thing to have rented: traffic flowed around it smoothly and without comment; police ignored it; passersby ignored it; and it made Andy and me invisible as we worked around it, so we could half work and half watch my landlord, his customers, his Doberman, his employees, without ourselves being seen. If we hadn't had the container, we couldn't have stood there for three minutes without someone asking us to state our business. The best part was when the girls from St. Alphonsus High School came by practically in formation—they were extremely pleasant to look at. We carried down all the rubbish I had been trying to get rid of for months and packed the container up to the top, and the next morning I woke up and saw the street in front of my building beautifully blank with the blankness of removed difficulties.

(1977)

COPS

I have seen the sun only about eleven times this summer, but every evening I lie on my bed and watch the sunset in the changes of light on my bedroom wall, on the door that opens from my bedroom onto the fire escape, and on the wall of the church behind my building. The door, when it is open, faces west, and in its window I can see reflected the cross-hatching of the fire escape, the roof of a building with a TV aerial on it, and, beyond that, actual sky (although not a part of the sky that is in any way center ring during sunsets). I enjoy thinking, as I watch, about all the things that are going on across the country at this time of day: uncoordinated Little Leaguers standing in various right fields praying that the ball will not be hit to them; girls sitting on front stoops waiting for dates; young men barbecuing steaks while annoying the house cats with water from the spray bottles used to keep the charcoal flames down; freight trains moving out of Laramie, Wyoming; people water-skiing on lakes that become calm at the end of the day. I also enjoy picking certain colors I see and figuring out what they would look like out of the context of the sunset. The corner of the window ledge on the church wall, for example, often turns a color during the more orange part of midsunset that could be closely duplicated by a rectangle of fresh muskmelon, and the part of my white bedroom wall farthest from the door is the color of pink skin seen through white cotton. The clouds reflected in the door are sometimes the color that, when I used to paint houses, was called Governor's Palace Tan, in a sky of Howard Johnson's blue. Toward the end of a good sunset, there is usually a color so pervasive that I could not get the necessary distance on it to name it or compare it to anything until one evening at the right time a friend of mine was over, looked at my back door and my bedroom wall, and said, "Oh! How mauve!"

On a recent Sunday night, the sunset shut down early. Olive-drab clouds moved in and made everything look like the bottom of the East River. Leaving my back door open, I went over to my couch and turned on *Hee Haw*. Just as Buck Owens had started singing his version of "Lodi," a voice from my back door said, "Sir?" I was startled; no one had ever come to my back door before. It was dark enough to use my flashlight, and I walked toward the door. The first thing my flashlight picked up was a gun, pointing down. The light traveled up the arm and came to a blue short sleeve with the New York Police insignia on it. I stepped onto the fire escape, and there was a hatless, partly bald policeman with vertical lines of sweat in the middle of his shirt, front and back.

"Did you hear anybody run up this fire escape?" he asked.

I said that I hadn't heard anybody but that the TV had been on.

"*Goddam!*" he said. He was holding his .38 as casually as if it were a telephone receiver, and he was panting. "You sure?"

I said I was sure, and he climbed down from my fire escape to the roof of the burglar-alarm store next door, and then he jumped the one story from that roof down into the alley between the store and another one-story building, landing flat-footed with an expulsion of breath. He walked to the chain-link fence at the street end of the alley, climbed over it, and then leaned against it on the other side, resting the wrist of his gun hand on the small of his back as he peered down the alley. I came back into my apartment, went out onto my front fire escape, and watched him.

"Go up a couple of flights and see if you can see anybody on that roof," he said, pointing to a building at the end of the block.

I climbed up two flights and saw my upstairs neighbor talking on the phone with his bed light on as I passed his window. I couldn't see anything else.

The policeman's partner came over. They conferred; they went to the patrol car. Sirens started in the distance. A police van rolled up. Then a police truck. Then a very large green-and-white police truck came. Policemen were all over the sidewalk. Many of them were wearing blue baseball caps, like the SWAT teams on TV. They started bringing shotguns out of the vehicles and loading them from boxes of shells, six shells per gun. They took an extension ladder out of the big truck. They took chain cutters out of the smaller truck. One of the policemen tried to cut the lock off the chain-link fence but couldn't. Another policeman took the cutters from him and cut the lock off. They brought the ladder into the alley and fooled around with it for a while, finally getting it up to about its full extension. Then three policemen with loaded shotguns climbed the ladder onto the roof of the building on the other side of the alley, and from that roof to the roof of the building at the end of the block. Five other policemen, two using flashlights with battery packs the size of family Bibles, began to go through some scrap metal in the far corner of the alley. Several more policemen stayed on the street.

"Hey, Vic!" one of the men on the roof called down. "What is this guy, anyway?"

"Male, black, six-two, and he doesn't have any shirt on!" one of the policemen on the ground called back.

I could see the policemen on the roof opposite clearly enough to observe that their hands were far up the barrels of their shotguns, on the pumps. They were creeping. The policemen in the alley found a broken pane of glass in one of the windows of the church, big enough to suggest that someone could have crawled through. The policemen on the roof began to climb around on the scaffolding of a billboard up there. I had looked at the billboard many times, but I had never realized before that you could climb on it, or how hard it is to see a person when he climbs on it.

After a while, the policemen in the alley came back onto the street, and the policemen on the roof came down. They stood around on the street, many of them with their shot-

guns on their shoulders. I saw the glows from several cigarettes. I heard laughter. Then they unloaded the shotguns,
collected the rest of their equipment, got into their police
vehicles, and drove away.

(1978)

CANAL STREET

Canal Street, in lower Manhattan, is the shortest route from an East River crossing to a Hudson River crossing on the island. To the east, Canal Street leads across the Manhattan Bridge, to Brooklyn; to the west, it leads into the Holland Tunnel, to New Jersey. Canal Street is actually an extension of Brooklyn's Flatbush Avenue and of any number of roads in New Jersey laid through the crooked alleys of downtown. The traffic on Canal Street never stops. It is a high-energy current jumping constantly between the poles of Brooklyn and New Jersey. It hates to have its flow pinched in the density of Manhattan, hates to stop at intersections. Along Canal Street, it moans and screams. Worn brake shoes of semi trucks go "Ooohhhh nooohhhh" at stoplights, and the sound echoes in the canyons of warehouses and Chinatown tenements. People lean on their horns from one end of Canal Street to the other. They'll honk nonstop for minutes at a time, until the horns get tired and out of breath. They'll try different combinations: shave-and-a-haircut, long-long-

long, short-short-short-long. Some people have musical car horns; a person purchasing a musical car horn seems to be limited to a choice of four tunes—"La Cucaracha," "Theme from *The Godfather*," "Dixie," and "Hava Nagila." Eventually, the flow of traffic knocks over everything upright along its route—mailboxes, fire hydrants, light poles, signs. Litter, fruit, rats, pigeons, and hats it flattens and pulverizes. Smaller pieces of metal it presses into the asphalt and makes two-dimensional. House keys, safety pins, gaskets, pop-tops, bottle caps, watch gears, buckles, umbrella ribs, alligator clips, and oil-paint tubes (many artists have studios nearby) shine dully in the pavement. When the traffic lets up a little—on the weekends, in the early morning—men working on the street with jackhammers erect barricades and break up the asphalt and throw it and its collection of lost objects into Dumpsters and cart it away.

At either end of Canal Street, billboards on the sides of buildings take a last shot at the traffic before it gets by. Canal Street is a gantlet of billboards and signs; Courvoisier, Pearl Paint, Bally's Grand Hotel, Salem Cigarettes, Lincoln Savings Bank, McDonald's, and signs in Chinese impend on the traffic, which is covered with signs and graffiti itself. A white panel truck with "Lust" graffitied on its side in black cuts off a Floors by Palumbo van and gets a horn blast in the back. Perk Up, Inc., of Tarrytown, gives a blast to Budget Rent-A-Truck; Taglianetti's Furniture Delivery Service blasts Palmieri Truckmen of Brooklyn; Firebird Freight stops inches from Basic Leasing Corp. ("WE LEASE DISHWASH-ERS AND ICE MAKERS") and emits a bellow of rage. A yellow moving truck with the motto "ON THE MOVE SINCE 1873" stalls in an intersection through several changes of the light as horn blasts bounce off its side. Weekly, the billboards flicker and change. Signs painted on buildings cover each other, fade, fall in flakes, reappear. Billboards shed strips of paper. One night, the car-burglar-alarm store near the corner of Canal and Thompson began to burn when Tony, the guy who sleeps in the store, apparently set fire by accident to a dish of rubbing alcohol in which he was soaking his earring studs, and suddenly flames were all around him, and he dived out under the security gate, which he could get only half open, and soon flames were shooting clear across the sidewalk, and the Fire Department came, and Tony was shivering on the street in a Black Sabbath T-shirt among the hoses saying, "I know I'm fired. I've already accepted that," and I brought from my apartment an old down vest and gave it to him, and he said, "Hey, this is comfortable. How much do you want for it?" and we stood and watched as the flames reached the big letters "AUTO ALARMS" on the top of the store, and they began to burn smokily, and the firemen on the roof knocked them off with axes, and they fell to the sidewalk and burned themselves in scrambled order into the chalk-white cement.

I lived two doors down, in a loft above an army-navy-surplus store. The next night, burglars came through the burned-out building, climbed our back fire escape, got into a second-floor storeroom, and stole several boxes of boots— all left feet, as it turned out. When my landlord, the proprietor of the army-navy-surplus store, learned this last fact, he

19

was almost happier than if he hadn't been robbed in the first place. The landlord is from Romania. His first name is Hugo, but he calls himself Gary; once I asked him where he got that name, and he said, "A chick gave it to me." Gary is Jewish, but he has an alternative set of business cards printed with an Arabic-sounding alias to give to people who might not like Jews. The surplus American Army shirts he wears at work generally have a name like "McCoy" or "Seagraves" over the breast pocket. When people he doesn't want to talk to come into his store looking for the owner, he tells them, "The owner is in Africa."

The unit of exchange on Canal Street is the dallah. Dallahs are dollars crossbred with dinars, pesos, yen, dirhams, zlotys, rubles, piastres. Salesmen in storefronts and sidewalk venders who know almost no other English yell "Fifty dallah!" and "T'ree dallah!" and "Ten dallah!" up and down the street. Dollars often exist only on paper or video display terminals; dallahs are always real. Dallahs are green, of small denomination, faded, crumpled, marked with ink and duck sauce and fingerprints and smears of blood. Dollars are carried in a bankbook or a wallet; the proper way to carry dallahs is in the right-front pants pocket in a folded wad with a red rubber band around it. When I ask Gary to lend me forty, he says, "Take sixty." He pulls his wad from his pocket and peels off three twenties. Then he stands looking at me with his eyebrows raised and his thumb poised above the bills, in case I might want more. He says, "All you got to do is ask." He says now if he gets robbed that's sixty he won't lose. Dallahs suggest robbery. To defend against it, Gary takes elaborate measures, which include surrounding himself with Doberman pinschers named Prince and Contessa and a rottweiler named Spirit. Prince is Gary's favorite. One day, Gary and Prince chased a suspected shoplifter from his store into a deli, where I was standing in the checkout line. Prince was hanging from the guy's sleeve, and Gary was beating the guy's head with a varnished brown billy club. The expression on Gary's face looked like one you might make to frighten a child. He was screaming from down in his throat. Shortly afterward, Prince was stolen. A photograph of Gary with tears in his eyes holding up a reward check for a thousand dollars for the return of his dog appeared on page 4 of the *Post*. The next day, Prince was returned by a man who took the precaution of arriving with a police escort. Gary asked how much he wanted, and he said he'd take five hundred. Gary wrote him a check.

Canal Street, which jury-rigs Brooklyn to New Jersey, is the place to go if you want to jury-rig something. Stores on Canal Street sell a lot of duct tape, extension cords, plastic sheeting to put over your windows in the winter, stapling guns, twine, plastic wood, miracle glues, quick-drying epoxy resins, and multiplug connectors. The street carpenters all kinds of shaky combinations. In hot weather, the passing traffic with its windows down blasts from many speakers a mixture of songs, like a radio dial being spun. Near the corner of Canal and Broadway is a store that used to sell luggage, jewelry, and take-out Chinese food but now just sells luggage. Another store sells plastic sheeting and imitation classical statues made of fiberglass. The nymphs and dryads and goddesses are displayed out front, chained to a security grate with bicycle locks around their necks. At Christmas, an automotive store at Canal and Hudson used to run a string of Christmas lights through the coils of razor wire above the fence surrounding its collection of old tires. Gary is not big on Christmas decorations. One year at Christmas he hung a white dove above the cash register from a strip of flypaper. Gary's store used to be as hodgepodge as any on Canal Street, with bins of gay and straight porno books, Statue of Liberty paperweights, needle-nose pliers, and underwater wrist compasses for skin divers. Now he sells mainly army-navy surplus and survival gear. Among his most popular items are defused Second World War hand grenades. He sells two kinds—good and rusty. Sometimes I could hear him calling on the loudspeaker to an assistant in the storeroom beneath me, "Danny. Bring me two *good* hand grenades, and two *rusty* hand grenades."

Some of what I know about Gary: he is forty-three years old; he lost relatives in the Holocaust; he spent a happy childhood in Israel, with a car, girls, trips to the beach; he lived for a time on a youth kibbutz, where boys occasionally swam naked with American girls; he moved without his family from Israel to New York to Canada; he once had a job in Toronto making the molds for three different sizes of Tek plastic toothbrush handles; he is handy with locks; he moved back to New York after his family moved there from Israel; he likes living in Forest Hills, Queens, because every morning on his lawn he sees ("Danny, what are those things I see in my yard, that I like?") squirrels; he has two brothers, one who manufactures corrugated-cardboard boxes and one who has been a caretaker-cashier in an S&M club; he works six or seven days a week, from ten in the morning to seven at night; he smokes cigars so strong that I could smell him coming up the stairs; he wears a little gold hand grenade on a chain around his neck; he likes to eat yellow rice from the Cuban restaurant, and it leaves a mustache; he has no real laugh, just a loud bark of sarcasm, triumph, or joy; his father was a scrap-iron dealer named Leo. I got to know Gary a first day of the month at a time, as I brought him my rent. One April 1 or October 1, he said to me, "I should get married—it's time." He began to subscribe to a publication called *Jewish Singles*, which he received at our building. One night, a friend who was visiting me saw *Jewish Singles* by the mail slot as he was leaving, took it home, and then called me to read me excerpts. I made him bring it back. At a dance, Gary met an American girl some years younger than he, and they were married. They named their first son Leo, after Gary's late father. Leo is now nine. Gary says, "When I bring him to Canal Street, I want to attach him to me by handcuffs."

On sunny weekends, Gary's store is so crowded that you have to turn your shoulders sidewise and sidle through. Gary's men Danny, Ezra, Mark, Kabul, Jeff, Eric, Walter, and Abbas watch the crowds. Customers Gary especially mistrusts do their shopping surrounded by his men, more or less in custody. From a raised step behind the cash register, Gary says to me, "See those bleck guys—they're t'ieves. If you ever see those guys around here, call the police. Danny. Abbas. Will you help these gentlemen, please? That white guy, with the earring, he's a junkie. He beats that girlfriend with the sexy T-shirt. He wanted me to sell him some Mace, I said, 'I'll sell Mace to her, not to you.' The Japanese kid there—A number one. Japanese A number one people in the *world*. He will spend a hundred and fifty dallah, at least. Japanese, I kiss their foot. That guy with the hat, he's a lawyer, a Hasidim. He's a rich guy, he don't want to share, always wants me to give him some kind of deal. He's hungry, like a typhoon. That other guy's a lawyer, too. He's sharp, are you kidding me? He's English, like the Beatles. (Yes, Zippo lighter, best lighter you can buy, it will burn for twenty years. Don't forget your brochure. Thank you.) That big guy? With the big hands, like baseball gloves? He's Russian, came over to Brighton Beach ten years ago, now he's the toughest landlord, the best landlord, in New York. Compared to him, I'm like a baby sheep. When the tenants don't pay the rent—POW!—he smacks them in the head. Russians don't play, you know. See those two guys? Out on the street? They'll come in in a minute. They're Arabs—PLO. They speak Yiddish ten times better than me. They buy a lot of stuff here—clothes, equipment—but no knives or nothin'. I know they would probably kill me, but then business is business."

Although the people Gary is talking about are only a few feet away, they don't hear him. Gary not only speaks several languages—Romanian, English, Yiddish, Hebrew, Greek, some Turkish, some Arabic, some Spanish—but also speaks in several frequencies. He has different channels for conversations with suppliers, customers, employees, and members of his family. In situations where he does not want to use words at all, he resorts to an ultrahigh frequency consisting of eye gestures, winks, and headshakes. These signs might mean Yes, No, Shut up, Look out, or I'll explain later. One day, some atmospheric scientists down in Delaware were performing cloud-seeding experiments on a thunderstorm and perhaps the storm got away from them because one came up the coast and hit New York City at about eight in the morning and dropped more rain than had ever fallen on the city on that date in the history of weather reporting. I was lying on my bed looking out my back door at the fire-hose stream coming from the broken drainpipe of the neighboring building and listening to the rain on the fire escape when suddenly I realized that some of the falling-water sound was coming from inside my apartment. I got up and saw water coming through my ceiling everywhere. I was on the third floor, with two floors above me. I ran to the roof, which is flat and bordered by a waist-high wall, and found it knee-deep in water. I ran down and got Gary, and we waded back onto the roof, and he reached his arm into a drain up to the shoulder and fished some trash out of the filter, and the water formed a big whirlpool and roared down the drain. A few moments later, we heard small cries from the street. The storm drain in the building's basement, unable to take such a volume of water, had instantly backed up, and two guys working in a little room down there had almost drowned in the flood. Thousands of dollars' worth of stuff Gary had stored in the basement was ruined. The tenant on the fifth floor, a costume designer, lost a lot of property, including several life-size frontal male-nude portraits, which he valued at some thousands of dollars each. The costume designer asked Gary to pay for the damage. Gary called his insurance man, who came by and took a tour of the costume designer's apartment with an expressionless face. Back on the street, he said to Gary, "Did you get a load of those naked guys!" and he began to laugh. The insurance company supposedly refused to pay for all the damage. Gary offered the costume designer a smaller amount than he had asked for. The costume designer refused it and sued Gary. Gary sued him back. Gary offered him money to leave, and he also refused that. One afternoon, someone broke into the costume designer's apartment and slashed up what remained of his stuff. The costume designer said he was sure Gary was responsible, and I said I could see how he might think that. Gary called me into his store and said, "How could you *say* such a thing, I would never *do* such a thing." I said, well, okay, but now I was worried about my apartment. How did I know a break-in like that wouldn't happen to me? With the tiniest of gestures, just between me and him—a slight downturning of the corners of the mouth, a hooding of the eyes, a shake of the head—Gary indicated that it wouldn't.

Before Gary bought the building, in 1976, it was the Knickerbocker Candy factory. Some of its pipes ran caramel, and there were gobs of crystallized caramel on the walls. When I moved in, my floor still had hundred-pound sacks of imitation coconut flakes lying around, no john, and no door. Back then the rent was $325 a month. Strangers used to walk in and ask me how much rent I was paying, and when I told them they would laugh in my face. Now a rent that low in this neighborhood would be unheard of. At first, I used the john at the Mobil station across the street. Then I hired a guy named Larry to install a bathroom. Larry was from Brooklyn, and he said he remembered visiting this building on a field trip when it was a candy factory and he was a kid in elementary school. He charged me $800, which I asked my mother for. She said she would be glad to help, and when I said how much I needed, her mouth dropped open. But afterward she gave me a check, enclosed in a greeting card. For a few years, I had just a bathroom and a bed and a phone—no kitchen, no TV or stereo. In the blackout of '77, I hunted all over the floor in the dark for the ringing phone, and when I found it, it was my mother calling to be sure I was all right. Eventually, I put in a new floor, so that it was possible to walk without shoes on, and a kitchen, and walls around the bathroom. The neighborhood, meanwhile, was getting tonier and tonier, and rents were climbing, and I could see Gary calculating. I had a five-year lease, but after three years I told Gary that I could afford to pay more. I said that from then on I would pay $150 a month more. Gary's eyes softened with wonder and love. To this day, he says, "Sandy, you don't know what you did to me. You touched me here"—with a finger to his sternum, next to the name tag that says "McCoy."

At the time, people told me I was crazy to raise my own rent. But it turned out to be one of the smartest things I've ever done. After the flood, the building entered a long period of feuds, suits, and countersuits, which I was able to stay out of. The feud between Gary and the costume designer went on for years. The guy on the fourth floor—below the costume designer, above me—also sued Gary over the water damage, and Gary alleged in a countersuit that the trash that had clogged the roof drain and created the whole problem had been left there by that guy in the first place, when he used to lie on the roof and sunbathe. Because just a single layer of boards constituted both my ceiling and that guy's floor, I knew him well, although we rarely spoke. I could hear when his cat jumped off his kitchen counter. The fights the guy had with women no amount of pillows on my head could drown out. Sometimes he and the women threw crockery at each other, and shards rained down on me through holes in my ceiling. The guy was a technician for a television studio when he moved in, but later he became possibly a drug dealer, possibly some other kind of criminal. His telephone rang nonstop. Once, it rang so long it made me fret and start to pace around. I decided to time it, and the continuous rings went on for twenty minutes, thirty minutes, forty. I was now breathing hard and talking to myself. I stood up on a ladder and looked through a hole in the floor. By standing on tiptoes I could just make out his phone, ringing away on the wall. I happened to have a long section of half-inch copper pipe, which the plumber had left, and experimentally I pushed it through the hole, past his chair, past his kitchen counter, past his dish drainer. The pipe was just long enough to reach the bottom of the phone receiver. I lined everything up as if this were a long pool shot. With a little tap, I knocked the phone off the hook, and it swung and dangled from its cord. The silence was sweet. Then I began to feel guilty. I wrote the guy a note explaining what I had done, and left it on his door. I heard him come home at about three in the morning, I heard him unfold the note, I heard him laugh. A few minutes later, a note slid under my door. The guy was a fan of Pauline Kael, and she had heavily influenced his prose style. He said he imagined the building's plumbing in "a macabre, twilight zoney revolt of anthropomorphic metals." I couldn't think of anything to respond, and did my best to avoid him for the next several years.

Walking east on Canal Street from Gary's building, you might have passed an electronics store with a pile of computers in the trash out front and a man picking through the pile, yanking out panels of circuitry like honeycombs from a hive; a onetime nice diner now taken over by heaps of VCRs and clock radios and radar detectors in cardboard boxes sold at cut rates by a family of Moroccan Jews who wear headphones outside their knit caps and park illegally during rush hour and litter the sidewalk with packing material and call their store "Big Zubby," which means something dirty in Arabic; the 3 Roses Bar, which changed the color of its crêpe-paper decorations for each holiday and which used to be filled with black working people and then began to attract young white people and then moved to 311 Church Street; a flea market in the parking lot next to the post office with gilt picture frames priced at five dollars each accidentally framing the Day-Glo graffiti on the wall behind them; Uncle Steve, a TV-and-stereo store where the owner did his own radio commercials, which ended "I lo-o-o-o-ve you"; Ollie (Something), a tall West Indian man in a leather skullcap who sold old record albums and old copies of *Playboy*; the intersection of Canal and Broadway, a famous intersection, which has appeared on television, in movies, and in a realistically detailed sculpture by Red Grooms now on display at the Cleveland Museum of Art. In the next block, Chinatown begins. The Excellent Dumpling House, near the corner of Canal and Lafayette, announces it with the ozone smell of oil heating in a wok. If the time is between October and New Year's, Christmas carols in Chinese are playing from the leather-goods, makeup, jewelry, and videotape store by the Lexington Avenue IRT subway entrance. Carp show the red of their gills as they gasp in the milky water of a big metal tank in a seafood store at the corner. One carp swims upside down.

Farther on, you might have seen Chinese vegetable stands, with their crates of non–supermarket produce—lotus root, and white carrots, and green carrots, and Chinese chives, and water chestnuts, and wrinkled bitter melons—which the people who work there are sick of telling tourists the names of; a store that sells mostly shellfish and has a wooden counter full of sea-colored lobsters writhing in very slow motion beneath a sign saying "$6.50 LB, NO PICTURES"; sidewalk venders selling live crabs and assorted mushrooms and pieces of dried shark stomach; a sign advertising the House of Watch; lots of jewelry stores, with clerks in the windows arranging necklaces on velvet stands shaped like headless necks; black security guards in front of the jewelry stores flirting with women wearing gold charms in the shape of the Dominican Republic; a shopping arcade where (according to *The Times*) young ethnic-Chinese refugees from Vietnam hang out between errands of extortion against local businesses, which they perform for the Chinatown gangs. Police think some of the refugees belong to a gang that killed two members of another gang in 1988 near 269 Canal. If the time is between Memorial Day and the Fourth of July, Chinese kids and Italian kids wearing white shorts, sneakers, no shirts, and towels around their necks try to sell you fireworks. The sidewalk here is narrow and polished smooth by feet. Some days, the crowds are so thick that people come to a complete stop and stand and wait.

Just beyond the intersection of Canal and the Bowery, across an asphalt expanse of traffic lanes and concrete dividers and yellow stripes painted on the pavement, is the arch at the entrance to the Manhattan Bridge. Traffic going to and coming from the bridge drives on ramps around long, columned wings extending from either side of the arch. Depending on the time of day, traffic going one direction or the other drives under the arch itself. The arch is maybe forty feet high, embellished with goddesses of victory, shields, fasces, tridents, spears, flags, helmets, winged lion heads. Across the top of the arch, in bas-relief, is a frieze of Indians on horseback hunting buffalo. The Indians draw their bows all the way back among a galloping herd of adults and calves. One horse prances on its hind legs. At the keystone of the arch, a buffalo head looks down on the tops of passing trucks. An afterthought of twin steel cables stretched from one leg of the arch to the other holds yellow traffic-signal boxes. Along the wings of the arch, in between the columns, people with no place to live store folded-up cardboard cartons, plastic bags of clothes, a laundry cart, sneakers, a broom. Sometimes sanitation men come along and clean this out, and then all that is left, on a ledge at the base of a column, is a single plastic vial of those scented oils people sell in the subway. Windrows of trash pile up on one side of the traffic dividers that route the cars coming off the bridge. As you approach, pigeons leap from the trash like flames.

Actually, Canal Street does not stop at the bridge but angles off to the east for eight blocks. Here it is not an artery but just a Lower East Side street. Guys lie in it to work on their cars. The gutter holds blue safety glass from a shattered car window, birdseed, a squashed gherkin, puddles of fluorescent-green radiator coolant. Nobody yells at trucks that double-park. A Chinese man standing at the back of a truck loads garments that come to him down a long cord strung directly from the truck to a window on the top floor of a nearby building. Pastel sports shirts on hangers descend one after another in five-story swoops. On this part of Canal Street, Chinese businesses mix with kosher delis, locksmiths, upholstery stores, and Hasidic hardware stores, which are closed on Saturday. Just below Canal is a network of narrow streets centuries older than the bridge roaring above them. It is Chinatown, but not the part where conventioneers come to eat Chinese food. Some of the side streets are so narrow they barely have curbs, much less sidewalks. Flatiron buildings almost small enough to put your arms around occupy tiny wedge-shaped lots. Gentrification has left this place untouched; rents here are probably about the same as they were in Carthage, or Nineveh, or Peking under the Tangs. Shoes have worn shallow depressions in the stone of apartment-house steps; hands have polished the paint off railings. Ancient paint on door lintels is cracked and ridged like alligator hide. This is the basic city that people have always lived in, of which the rest of New York is only the twentieth century's approximation. Market Street, which runs parallel to the bridge just south of it, angles down to the blue of the East River like a lane in a seacoast town.

In the Sun Sing Theatre, on East Broadway directly under the bridge, in the middle of the day, two dozen Chinese men in white short-sleeved shirts are watching a movie about the adventures of a fisherman from mainland China who comes to visit his more sophisticated relatives in Hong Kong. Outside, little kids with backpacks and with the hoods of their jackets drawn tight around their faces run to meet their mothers. Some teenage kids walk by singing a song about you've tried the rest, now try the best. Big yellow Chinese characters painted on the sidewalk translate as "Seriously no park car." In a store on Henry Street filled with small, bright birds in wooden cages, two men unroll and discuss an illuminated Chinese scroll. Sparrows on a fire escape across the street answer the birds singing through the open door. A few doors down, guys in red smocks are laughing in a printing store that sells mainly Chinese-restaurant menus. A boy goes by wheeling a long-haired white cat in a wheelbarrow. At the corner, a woman cobbler has set up her bench. She bends over and saws at the heel of a burgundy leather boot while its wearer holds on to a street sign for balance. A mounted Norman Rockwell print of a red-cheeked cobbler leans against the wall nearby.

Walking west on Canal, away from Chinatown, toward the Hudson River, you can understand why people who drive this street become so upset. In the course of its half mile or so, they are going a long way—from the Old World to the New, or vice versa. If the eastern end of Canal Street is Nineveh, its western end is Brasília. When you head in this direction, each intersection seems a little less ethnic than the one before it, and there is a scent of the American continent up ahead. At certain times of year, the red sun sets right at the end of the street. Westward, the buildings get bigger and farther apart, with growing vistas of sky between. The light and the space probably tempt drivers to think they are about to soar onto one of those empty skyways of the car commercials, when in fact they're not. At the river, just beyond the cars speeding by on the West Side Highway, the island ends like a piece of paper on a table. A plaza at the foot of Canal is empty except for some cars and a collection of snowplow attachments the city has lined up in rows. Fewer horns honk here. On the opposite bank, you can see the lights of Jersey City and Hoboken and farther upstream. The water is unoccupied, the sky as big as any in Manhattan. Eighty years ago, right at the river's edge is where the worst traffic jam was, as cars, trucks, and horse-drawn wagons waited to get on the several ferries across. The sky and the water here used to be almost invisible for the piers and shipping warehouses. Now a few splintery pilings are about all that remains. As the sun goes down, the sky becomes a darker blue, and you can make out the lights of airplanes at different altitudes above Newark Airport.

Westbound traffic on Canal Street does not soar but instead descends slowly three blocks from the river into the entrance to the Holland Tunnel. Few tunnelbound cars have any passengers besides the driver. Guys prop the *Post* on the steering wheel and read as they wait to roll the next few feet. Traffic reports on the radio sometimes predict delays of over an hour. Weighted yellow cylinders hanging from a cable just before the tunnel entrance bump the top of any truck taller than twelve feet six inches, and an electric eye sets warning bells ringing and brings a cop running from a little booth. A sign above the entrance says "12'6" WE MEAN IT!" In fact, clearance in the tunnel is thirteen-six, but the tunnel authorities leave themselves an extra foot in case a broken vehicle needs to be jacked up for repairs. Trucks roar and creak their way into the tunnel, and give off enough exhaust to make the air here some of the most heavily polluted in the city. Set back in a niche at the tunnel entrance, like a man eternally waiting to cross, is a bronze bust of Clifford Milburn Holland, the engineer who designed the tunnel and worked himself to death building it.

Clifford Holland was born in 1883, in Somerset, Massachusetts. Among his ancestors were Puritan ministers who came to New England in the 1600s. Holland graduated from the Cambridge Latin School in 1902, worked his way through Harvard, got a degree there in civil engineering in 1906, and came to New York to work on tunnels. As tunnel engineer with the Public Service Commission, he built four double-tube subway tunnels under the East River that the BMT trains run through. In 1919, partly to relieve traffic congestion downtown, a new agency called the New York and New Jersey Vehicular Tunnel Commission decided to build a tunnel under the Hudson River, from Canal Street to Twelfth Street in Jersey City. They hired Holland as chief engineer to design and build it. At the time, Holland was probably the country's leading expert in the shield method of tunnel construction. This method uses a steel-plate cylinder, or shield, which is driven into the earth by powerful jacks at its back edge while men remove the rock and the dirt in the middle. As the shield advances, a tunnel wall of iron rings is set in place behind. One benefit of the method is that the shield can be divided into sealed compartments and filled with compressed air to counteract the pressure of water; that allows subaqueous tunneling through wet substances like silt. The bottom of the Hudson is many feet deep in tiny particles of granite, sand, and basalt eroded from the rocks along its banks—"plain, black mud," as Holland described it. Holland's plan called for two parallel tunnels, one for eastbound traffic and one for westbound. In October of 1922, the first shield began digging toward New Jersey from the intersection of Canal and West streets. The joint tunnel commission had budgeted twelve million dollars for the project and paid Holland a starting salary of ten thousand dollars a year.

The Holland Tunnel was the first tunnel in the world designed for motor traffic. Holland and his staff spent a lot of time finding a way to get combustion gases out of the tunnel and finally devised a system using ventilating shafts, giant blowers, and ducts below the roadway and in the ceiling for outgoing and incoming air. Like many of the automobile drivers in the Canal Street traffic jam today, Holland was a commuter. He belonged to the first generation of men who drove to work from the suburbs in cars. Holland lived in Flatbush, in a three-story house with a yard and a driveway, at 2416 Avenue J. He had a wife, Anna, and four daughters—Anne, Clarissa, Venita, and Lydia. Lydia was only a year old when digging on the tunnel began. Today, Holland's old neighborhood is occupied mostly by Hispanics and Orthodox Jews. Crowds of strollers with clear plastic covers fill the crosswalks at eleven in the morning, and the only trash among the well-trimmed hedges is an empty bottle of a vitamin that claims to improve fertility. Nothing about 2416 distinguishes it from hundreds of other brick-and-stucco houses extending for miles along Avenue J.

There is no reason to expect that a man who built a famous tunnel should be remembered, or that the house his body was brought back to should have a plaque in the yard. The urge to tunnel is partly an urge to disappear, and its product, no matter how monumental, is visible only from the inside. People have written scores of books on the Brooklyn Bridge and its engineers, the Roeblings; the only book on the Holland Tunnel is a sixty-eight-page volume put out by the company that built the tunnel's ventilating fans. One of the authors of that book visited Clifford Holland inside the tunnel and described him joking and relaxing in the pressurized air of the shield's forward compartment while work went on around him. In photographs aboveground, Holland appears as an inconspicuous business-suited man of less than average height with a bullet-shaped head, sloping shoulders, and rimless spectacles. His body angles slightly away from the camera; he seems to blink in the light. It is hard to avoid the observation that he looks like a mole. "Head Mole" was how the newspapers sometimes referred to him. Tunnel workers liked him. Construction bosses said that Holland could persuade them to efforts that no one else could.

Digging tunnels is so difficult and dangerous and unlike other kinds of work that it amounts to a vocation. The laborers who do it call themselves sandhogs. Because of the physical demands of the job, and because the sandhogs often worked in the shield's forward compartment under air pressure up to fifty pounds per square inch, they had to pass regular physical exams. They were not supposed to be over thirty-nine, but many were. Working in pressurized air is enervating, and the sandhogs' union would not allow shifts of more than four hours; as the pressure went up, the shifts became shorter and the pay greater. The highest-paid sandhogs earned $8.50 a day. Under the river, beneath bare lightbulbs in the advancing shields, with the smoke of blasting hanging permanently in the gloom, and the racket of pneumatic grouting machines echoing off metal walls, the sandhogs picked and shoveled at the slaty gray bedrock. In this intense, pressurized atmosphere, a cigarette burned down to a butt in three puffs, and it was impossible to whistle. Entering or leaving pressurized air, the sandhogs had to pass through an air lock to accustom their bodies to the change. A sandhog who became impatient to go home and left the air lock too soon was liable to get the bends, a painful and occasionally fatal condition produced by bubbles of nitrogen in the blood, which could make him stagger as if drunk, fall down, and lose consciousness. Sandhogs wore medical ID bracelets around their wrists in case they should be overcome by the bends away from the job.

Sandhogs are a tribe, with their own rituals, myths, and hero tales. Many sandhogs are related to one another. Sitting in the air lock, or showering after their shift, or drinking in a sandhogs' bar, they tell stories. The favorite sandhog hero tales are about men who have been in blowouts and survived. A blowout is a catastrophic event in tunnel construction that occurs when the pressure of air inside the shield suddenly becomes greater than the water pressure in the material the shield is tunneling through. If the shield happens to hit a seam or a bubble or a weak spot underground, the pressurized air in the shield will sometimes blow right up through the river bottom, through the river, and into the sky in a tall geyser, taking men and equipment with it. Among the most famous sandhog heroes was a man named Marshall Mabey, who survived a blowout that shot him through yards of river bottom and onto the top of a geyser twenty-five feet above the East River during the construction of the IRT subway tube to Brooklyn in 1916.

When the Holland Tunnel was built, it was the longest subaqueous tunnel in the world. New York and New Jersey both ended up spending more money on it than they had ever spent on a local work before. The tunnel used 117,000 tons of cast iron from mills in Pennsylvania, hundreds of miles of steel reinforcing rods, 800,000 ten-pound bolts, 1.5 billion board-feet of lumber from Georgia and Oregon, steel-and-concrete caissons made in Staten Island, granite paving from New England, and concrete from Cementon, New York. It employed seventeen hundred men (including the undaunted Marshall Mabey). At the height of construction, six shields were digging the tunnel and its approaches—two shields heading west from Manhattan, two heading east from New Jersey to meet them, and two more digging land entrances in Jersey City. Work went on seven days a week, twenty-four hours a day. After spending all day at the site, Holland often came back in the evening to see how work was progressing.

In Manhattan, the work went slowly. The two shields—the second one began digging from the corner of Spring and West streets in April of 1923—took many months to go the few hundred feet from their starting points to the edge of the island. The problem was that their routes underground led not through natural mud or rock but through all kinds of miscellaneous landfill and rubbish that Manhattanites had been dumping along the edge of the island to enlarge it for over two hundred years. There were no records of when this land was filled or what it was made of, so Holland did not know what to expect. Mostly, the fill consisted of water-logged cribs of immense rough-hewn planks enclosing pilled-up heaps of granite in chunks. In the high air pressure needed to hold back the sand and the ooze, sandhogs sawed the wood and blasted the rocks. A canal that had been dug in 1805 to drain a pond where Foley Square is now—the canal that gave Canal Street its name—apparently also washed a lot of rock and brick and ancient refuse to the river's edge. Before or after the canal was covered over, in

1820, it was lined with bricks, to make the largest storm drain in the city. Holland had to reinforce these old bricks with iron plates as he tunneled carefully past. He also came within five feet of a cofferdam at a sewage-treatment plant at West Street, and almost as close to several gas lines, water mains, and electric cables. Some days, the shields moved forward only a few inches, or not at all. Holland said that every foot of tunnel progress in Manhattan was a new story.

On the New Jersey side, where sedimentary mud was hundreds of feet deep, Holland expected progress to be much more rapid. But there his biggest problems turned out to be aboveground, in the form of the New Jersey Interstate Bridge and Tunnel Commission. This group was half of the New York and New Jersey Vehicular Tunnel Commission. A nine-member commission from New York made up the other half. The two halves did not get along. The chairman of the New Jersey commission was a man named T. Albeus Adams. He praised the project with a speech to the effect that this tunnel would be like Lincoln's proclamation freeing the slaves, but even before digging had begun he was accusing the New York commissioners of denying him adequate desk space in the offices the commissions shared on Centre Street. This dispute continued for some time, until an acceptable desk was installed. A more serious argument had to do with the tunnel entrance in Jersey City. The New Jersey commissioners thought its design insultingly small; they wanted a big plaza and widened streets leading to it. The New Yorkers thought the Jerseyites were trying to improve their city unnecessarily at the tunnel's expense. Whenever the subject of street widening came up at joint commission meetings, people shouted and stalked out. Neither side would yield. New York prepared to sue New Jersey in federal court; New Jersey said that the governors should step in. Holland and a consulting engineer on the New Jersey commission devised a compromise plan for the plaza, which both sides seemed to accept. Then the commissioners disagreed about the construction in the plaza of a ten-thousand-dollar stone-and-bronze monument honoring both commissions, which New Jersey said was New York's idea and New York said was not. The delay continued. Finally, Holland and a small crew secretly went out to Jersey City just before dark one evening and broke ground for the tunnel themselves. One of the Jersey commissioners referred to this as a "contemptible, mean trick" seven times at a commission meeting. Later, when workmen tried to do further tunnel construction on the Jersey side, the Jersey City police stopped them for not having the proper permit. Eventually, months behind schedule, work in New Jersey did begin. The joint tunnel commission had long planned an elaborate formal groundbreaking there, with ten thousand guests and President Harding to attend. When the time came, the two sides of the river were so fed up with each other that the celebration was canceled.

After tunneling through Manhattan landfill all winter, the shield that had started from the intersection of Canal and West streets entered the silt at the bottom of the Hudson River. Here progress went five times as fast. When the shield was well out under the river, 1,113 feet from its starting point, it encountered a wall of rock extending in front of it for 800 feet. This rock was Manhattan schist, part of a formation that extends to the Jersey Palisades upstream. Progress again slowed, from twelve and a half feet a day to less than a foot. The shield digging the parallel tube west from Spring Street hit the same rock a month or so later. Because the rock face did not extend all the way to the ceiling of the tunnel, Holland had to be especially careful in gauging the force of the dynamite charges he used. The blasts had to be strong enough to break the rock without damaging the shield or disturbing the silt at the ceiling. Despite precautions, at 7:45 a.m. on April 3, 1924, water began streaming through a hole in the two feet of silt at the ceiling of the Canal Street tube. Sandhogs tried to stop the hole with bales of hay, but, in a sudden hiss of escaping air, it grew into a tear twenty feet long. As water gushed into the shield, a foreman, David Brown, shouted, "Run for your lives, men!" Thirty-five sandhogs scrambled through the shield's escape hatch and up the tunnel with the incoming river at their heels. Meanwhile, a fifty-foot geyser of compressed air shot through the hole and into the sky over the Hudson, nearly capsizing a cement barge. The sandhogs made it up the slope of the tunnel before the water, and no one was injured. Additional air pressure drove the water from the tube, and the hole in the river bottom was plugged with two bargeloads of clay.

In addition to solving engineering problems never before encountered in tunnel construction—such as anchoring a ten-thousand-ton caisson for the west ventilating shaft to bedrock through 250 feet of riverbed muck, and designing metal joints so the tunnel could move fractions of an inch with changes of temperature and the action of the tides—

Holland continually had to explain things. He had to explain why a concrete tunnel, championed by T. Albeus Adams, would probably float, and why two smaller tunnels were better than one big one, and how the money spent on the New Jersey entrance plaza was actually more than that spent on the Manhattan plaza, and why work was going so slowly in Manhattan, and why it made more sense to hire an experienced tunnel-construction firm rather than an inexperienced one championed by T. Albeus Adams, and why the tunnel was going to cost sixteen million dollars more than the original estimate (it eventually cost a total of forty-eight million dollars), and why he refused to allow an engineer hired at the urging of a New Jersey commissioner to leave work for a week to get out the vote for the Hudson County Democratic organization. Over and over, he explained to people worried about carbon-monoxide poisoning how the tunnel's ventilation system would work; when a traffic jam in a tunnel in Pittsburgh ended with hundreds in the hospital, he explained why that couldn't happen here. As the tunnels reached midstream, construction sometimes delayed the departures of cruise liners, to the annoyance of society swells on board. In detail, Holland explained the routes through the construction that cruise ships could take, and why the mounds of clay on the river bottom that they had to avoid were necessary to protect the workmen below.

By the late summer of 1924, the shields tunneling west from Manhattan were within a few hundred feet of the shields coming east from New Jersey. Everyone awaited the "holing through"—the moment when east and west shields would meet and the first tube would finally go all the way from one end to the other. Newspapers said that the tunnel was approaching its zero hour, and that the engineers were lying awake nights worrying that the meeting would not be exact. Tunneling simultaneously from both sides of the river, Holland was like a person drilling holes through opposite sides of a block of wood; if the holes didn't meet, the project would be ruined. Each shield had an instrument man who kept track of the shield's position inch by inch. Holland stayed in close touch with the instrument men to hold the shields exactly to line and grade. Once the hole was made, there could be no correction. Holland hoped for a margin of error of less than an inch. Despite a weak heart, which he had had since youth, he went in and out of pressurized chambers many times a day. His wife saw that the work was a strain on his health. "If I had known that it was sapping his strength so much, I would have urged him to be more careful," she said later, "but he was so completely wrapped up in his work that I really do not know if my pleadings would have had any effect." On September 27, the two shields digging the northern tube were within 165 feet of each other. A meeting was expected within a month. The first week in October, Holland had a nervous breakdown. The joint tunnel commission adopted a resolution giving him a month off with pay, and a second month if he needed it; uncharacteristically, no one dissented. Holland went to the Battle Creek Sanitarium, in Michigan. His friend Robert Ridgway, the chief engineer for the New York Board of Transportation, went to visit him a few weeks later, and Holland stayed up late talking about how much he wanted to finish the tunnel. Sad not to be returning himself, Holland saw Ridgway off at the train station. That night, Holland had a heart attack and died.

Two days later, the tunnel's northern tube was holed through. Again, the tunnel commissions had planned a celebration: the president (now Coolidge) would press a gold-and-platinum telegraph key in the White House library, which would touch off a blast removing the last eight feet of rock between the two halves of the tube; radio station WOR would broadcast the sound of the blast to the tristate area; a band would play "The Star-Spangled Banner"; governors and senators would observe. Out of respect for Holland, no celebration was held. All the workers decided to treat the event as part of an ordinary day. A few minutes after the blast, when the debris and the smoke had cleared, the New York superintendent of the work crawled through a small hole in the wall and shook hands with his counterpart from the Jersey side. The sandhogs did not cheer. When the remaining rock and mud were cleared away, it was found that the two borings diverged from each other by three-quarters of an inch.

Holland's body was brought back from Michigan to 2416 Avenue J, Flatbush, and after a memorial service in Brooklyn he was buried in Somerset, Massachusetts. In a letter to Governor Alfred E. Smith of New York, Theodore D. Pratt, the general manager of the Motor Truck Association of America, suggested that the new tunnel be named the Holland Tunnel. Soon afterward, the joint tunnel commission agreed to this idea, and the Hudson River Vehicular Tunnel (as it had been called) became the Holland Tunnel.

The southern tube was holed through a month after the northern tube. Anna Holland and her four daughters moved from Flatbush to Cambridge, Massachusetts. The tunnel's twin tubes were lined with concrete, ventilated, paved, tiled, lit, and opened for traffic at one minute after midnight on November 13, 1927.

When the tunnel commission hired Holland as engineer, in 1919, he had insisted that several men who had worked closely with him in the past be hired also. Milton Freeman, his second-in-command, who took over for Holland at his death, knew Holland's plans and methods so well that the work continued with no interruption. Freeman's dedication was at least as great as Holland's. "Mr. Freeman practically slept in the tunnel," Anna Holland recalled. On March 24, 1925, five months after becoming chief engineer, Milton Freeman died of acute pneumonia. The tunnel commission honored him by naming the Manhattan entrance plaza Freeman Square; today, that name has been forgotten. Holland's third-in-command, a man named Ole Singstad, took over from Freeman and survived to the end of the project. Besides Holland and Freeman, thirteen sandhogs died building the Holland Tunnel. *The Times* gave their names as Philip Healey, Steve Rolzek, Christopher Kelly, John Hues, Joseph Richard, G. J. Slade, Dennis Sullivan, John Taggart, Sezoy Palischick, Feodor Tarashicp, August Nevola, Charles Svenson, and James G. Godfrey. Other newspapers printed the same thirteen names but disagreed on some of the spellings. When the first shield began to tunnel west from Canal Street, Holland described the men "rejoicing as if we were giving a battleship its first spin." The men who built the tunnel had a rallying cry: "Ten minutes to New Jersey by wheel!"

As if Clifford Holland's profession, diffidence, and short life weren't enough, his name itself was the final guarantee of his anonymity. At the time the tunnel was named for him, editorial writers worried that people would think that the name had something to do with Holland the country. In later years, that happened. Today, almost no one knows who Clifford Holland was. When I asked where the name of the Holland Tunnel came from at Tunnel Discount Stationers, near the corner of Canal and Broadway, a guy behind the counter with a blue knit short-sleeved shirt and a mustache said, "I really couldn't tell you. Library'd be your best shot." When I asked at Tunnel Machinery Exchange, Canal and Wooster, a tall guy with a pockmarked face and a mustache said, "The name of the Holland Tunnel comes from the Dutch—no, you stumped me." When I asked at Tunnel Garage, Thompson and Broome streets, a guy with a gray-and-black knit shirt and a mustache said, "Ask at the tunnel. For us, it is a little difficult." A traffic cop at the intersection of Canal and Sixth said, "I couldn't tell you that one, pal. I sure couldn't." A fireman by the firehouse at Canal and Allen said, "I have no idea. I imagine from somewhere over in the Netherlands." A woman in a blue jacket and black slacks at Lee Nam Sneaker, 316 Canal, said, "Don't know. Sorry." A gray-haired woman in a gray sweater at the cash register at Canal Deli Grocery, Canal and Greenwich, said, "I never even t'ought about it, frankly." When I asked Gary in his store one afternoon, he didn't know, and he repeated the question to the shoppers at large. A tall Japanese tourist with white hair at his temples who was comparing pairs of American and Israeli military goggles said, "It was named for engineer."

A plaque beneath the bust of Clifford Holland at the westbound entrance describes the tunnel as "the underground highway which joins a continent to a city." Gary has been through the tunnel only a few times; he is of the city. When I moved to New York from Ohio, in 1974, I thought of myself as a person from the continent. I made a point of how "American" I was and spoke in a down-home accent that surprised my friends from the town I grew up in when they came to visit. I moved into Gary's building in the summer of '76, while the bicentennial celebration was going on. From my front fire escape I could see all the way down Canal to a tall, thin slot of scenery at its end—a rectangle of Hudson River, a stripe of New Jersey, a column of sky. When the Tall Ships parade went by, each mass of sails seemed to cross this view in an instant, like a tiger sneaking from one tree to another in a cartoon. Back then, my fire escape was the only part of the apartment that did not need work, and I spent a lot of time out there staring westward. The sight of a truck from Storm Lake, Iowa, or Cape Girardeau, Missouri, heading down Canal to the tunnel was enough to make me happy. By concentrating on the sun on a peaked roof of a building downtown, I could imagine the sun on the roof of a boathouse in Michigan or a picnic kiosk in Nebraska—places I believed I would rather be.

The farthest west Gary has ever been is Caesars Pocono Palace Resort, in Pennsylvania, ten miles off Interstate 80 and just across the New Jersey state line. He spent thirty-six hours there with his wife some years ago—the only vacation I have ever known him to take. In the opinion of boosters of Pennsylvania who have put up a billboard that says "PENN-SYLVANIA—AMERICA STARTS HERE" next to the interstate where it leaves New Jersey, Gary can say that he has been to America. His knowledge of its geography, however, is vague. The first time I told him I grew up in Ohio, he said, "Ohio, Michigan?" A large part of his America falls into an area known as Upstate. (Me): "I just came back from New Haven." (Him): "Oh—upstate?" In fact, his map of the country could be divided into thirds—Florida, California, and Upstate. When I sublet my place to my sister in 1982 and moved to Montana for three years, that name suddenly appeared on Gary's map—alone and remote at the end of a long causeway, and occupied only by me. He pronounced it "Mon-*tah*-na." Since I returned, he has forgotten that name. Now he calls it "the place you went to."

In Gary's mind, America beyond New York is a land of no headaches: no traffic jams, no eight-and-a-quarter sales tax, no public-transportation tax, no water bills, no fire inspectors, no building inspectors, no lawsuits, no burglar alarms ringing in the middle of the night. He probably thinks of it as a giant slumbering baby: he often tells me it is my country, not his, and he often tells me I am a baby. "Sandy, Sandy, you sit up in a room writing, you like a baby, you don't know"—about the things people do to each other, about the Holocaust, about people paying off insurance adjusters, about how to make women behave, about black people on welfare laughing at me, about what the Palestinians would do to Israel if they had a chance, about how the rest of the world is waiting to come over here and take everything I've got. He says, "You an American, so you straight. But the world is not straight, it's crooked."

While I stand talking to Gary—which I still do, often—people come in and ask for rattraps, martial-arts equipment, gold braid, Mussolini youth medals, Civil War forage caps, earplugs, gas masks, white mosquito netting, wires to keep pants cuffs straight, camouflage paint, police whistles, flare guns, handcuffs, and holsters for guns of every description. One guy wanted to bring his Uzi machine gun from the car to see if the holster would fit. Another guy wanted to talk flashlights. He told Gary he would give his right arm for a certain model of flashlight. Then he went on about different kinds of batteries, bulbs, buttons, cases, and techniques of manufacturing flashlight reflectors. After the guy left, I asked Gary if he had any idea what the guy was talking about. He said, "If I did, would I be here?"

Recently, a developer offered Gary two and a half million dollars for his building. This offer did not delight Gary, despite the fact that he paid sixty thousand for the building originally. He said he would need two and a half million to buy a new building on Canal, so what was the difference? I told Gary he should take the money. I asked, "Don't you have a dream of something you'd like to do?"

"I'll tell you my dream—you'll probably laugh. I'd like to go to the place you went to."

"Montana?"

"Mon-*tah*-na. Yes. I'd go there, in the trees, with peace and quiet and no headaches. Give me ten million, not two, I'll go to Mon-*tah*-na, you'll never hear of Gary again."

(1990)

BUMPIN'N

The staff at the Brooklyn Museum left a blank book for visitors' comments outside the exhibition "Frédéric Bazille: Prophet of Impressionism." Bazille, who shared a studio with Monet and Renoir in the 1860s, died, at twenty-eight, in the Franco-Prussian War, and his work is seldom shown. The exhibition opened last November and closed a couple of weeks ago; by then, the blank book was nearly full of comments. Here are some:

The Lynch family has enjoyed this particular visit with great joy. Thank you so much for keeping the "Arts" alive

He's here, he's queer, he's everywhere! Moving works, wonderful space

A treat for both the eye and mind

Ah, Formidable et Magnifique!

Wish I could get out to see this special exhibit—Mike Tyson

I think you should have wiffle ball tournaments in the ballroom.

Perhaps a "Quiet" sign near the video would help.

Like a daycare center 11/14 . . . Todlers screaming

Very interesting, he was quite immature

All Bassille Paints is naked people and dead animals. Yuck!

Materials of the earth work well in *his* fingertips.

I swear one recumbent figure was copied by Seurat for his work, the boy in the water with his hands disappearing under the rippling surface.

Bravo! Beautifully executed & a sensitive touching exhibit.

Bravo! Idiotic pretension and lousy painting

I didn't like it too much!!

Beautifully hung exhibition—most interesting—but where is portrait of family?

Not enough exchange of fresh air to make viewing comfortable

What a pity he left only a sense of what would come—

Big B loves it!

Weird—very wierd

This place is so cool Wolverine

This is a very, very good place you got here! *Cyclops!*

I kill you

Uncle Dave looks happy!

I liked it. It helped me learn about long ago.

Security Boys Are No GooD

I think it's a terrible shame that this exquisite jewel of a museum has been so neglected by the city and its wealthy donors

This Museum is Bumpin'n

I don't like it when the restorant is closed

May God (Me) Bless You! Jesus Christ

I'm from Poland and I like this museum

F. Bazille is not as familiar a name as his friends because he was not nearly as talented as them, I'm sorry to say. C'est la vie.

Time is never still—or there would be no Bazille.

The museum is poorly laid out. The floors were closed. We won't be back.

Good—who needs ya!

F. Bazille is an academic realist—not an impressionist.

Am greatly impressed—as was Cezanne (and others)

If you stand back you see more detail. I am ten and the perspective of the unfinished one is very interestive

Guy Miggins feels that there should be more Guanese Art

This, and most American Museums and Galleries of Art in General *must* Accredit more attention to *Cartoon Comics Idiom as an Artform*.

Too bad he's dead!

Save some pennies and turn down the Heat!

Danny Peckman, Keith Peck and Paul John Ross thot this museum is it. This is the pinicle of life. We have decided to stay here for the rest of our laborious lives. P.S. Fight the power.

. . . Very derivative of Manet & Courbet. Museums should also quote from dissenting critics

Why no Réunion de Famille? Some explanation as to why this key work is absent would have been welcome.

I greatly admired Bazille for his use of Black women in his work!

In the interests of accuracy, the word "preference" in the label for "Summer Scene" should be changed to "orientation." It's *not* a matter of choice!

I was kind of hot, but was too busy to take off my sweatshirt. I finally took it off! Fwweu!

An interesting show—but he is hardly a prophet of impressionism—he was still finding his own style. Once again futility & waste of war is proven

Every thing was Dope (Peace out!)

You need seats!! Older people come to see this exhibition . . .

We ♥ it so much we cut school to come here! Shhh!

I thought his work was dull and uninteresting

I had fun here

Jenn says its a dang shame that he died so young. Like a still death of a new birth

The note about the painting "La Toilette" mentions the European design of the garment held by the right hand figure. Well, that garment is very clearly Chinese, not European!

I like it here. and I like to come back another day

(1993)

FRIEND OF THE BUILDING

In the days after the explosion at the World Trade Center, I thought about George Willig, a hero of mine. On May 26, 1977, George Willig climbed the World Trade Center using homemade handheld clamping devices, which he inserted in the window-washing channels on the northeast corner of the South Tower. His three-and-a-half-hour climb from the ground to the roof stopped traffic, drew clouds of helicopters, and made him briefly famous. He was twenty-seven at the time and lived in Queens. Today, he lives, with his wife, in Woodland Hills, California, and is an independent real-estate appraiser. I called him on the phone.

"I was on vacation in Costa Rica when the explosion happened," he said. "I didn't read about it in the papers or see anything about it on TV. My wife called our answering machine, and there was a message from my mother-in-law saying there'd been a fire or a bomb or something at the World Trade Center. We got back on Monday, and I went out and got a Sunday *Times*, but I didn't get a chance to read it right away.

"People used to ask me about the World Trade Center all the time—refer to me as the Human Fly, and all that. But for a few years now I haven't talked about it much. Sometimes I'll remember the climb, and I'll ask myself, 'Did I really do that?' I'm a pretty modest person, and sometimes I find it amazing that I really did. I thought about making the climb for a year or more beforehand. I'm interested in research and development, and I saw it more as an engineering challenge. I worked out the details carefully, and I knew my plan was very secure and solid and I couldn't fall down. I picked that particular corner because I wanted a good view and I wanted New York to have a good view of me. I kept going back to the building and working out all the problems. I'd stop and say, 'What, am I crazy? Have I lost it?' And I'd rationalize that I wasn't going to do it, and then suddenly I'd think about it again and get this adrenaline rush. Now it seems like it was like falling in love—an inescapable attraction to someone or some thing. Like destiny.

"Looking around doesn't bother me when I climb, and I'm not afraid to look down. I started the climb about six-thirty in the morning, and I was pretty far up by rush hour. I took as many mental snapshots as I could. I could see cars stopped on the highway along the river, and quite a crowd below, and I saw the Fire Department, or somebody, blow up an air bag. It looked like the head of a pin—it wouldn't have been much use if I'd needed it.

"When I got to the top, I was arrested, of course, and the city said they were going to fine me a quarter of a million dollars. They ended up fining me a dollar and ten cents—a penny a floor. I went on a lot of talk shows and was in newspapers and on the radio, and I came out with a book. For a while there, I felt like I was a dollar sign with legs. Newspaper reporters who were writing about me found out that my mother had been trapped in the Empire State Building back in 1945, when the B-25 crashed into it. She was working for the Catholic War Relief Services, on the seventy-eighth floor, when the plane hit a floor above or below, and she saw a lot of smoke and flames, and her boss burned up. He came running to her on fire and told her to save herself, and she was sure she was dead, so she took off her school ring and a ruby friendship ring my dad had given her before he went overseas, and she threw them out the window. She said she thought it would be a shame to let them burn up, and she wanted someone else to have them. I remembered her telling me about that when I was five or six, but I hadn't thought much about it since. Newspapers started referring to my 'edifice complex.' I wouldn't have said it had anything to do with my climb, but now I think it's a pretty incredible coincidence.

"I haven't been back to New York in a couple of years. My wife and I will probably go this summer. As part of a publicity gimmick I did for the World Trade Center back in '77, the guy who ran the observation deck gave me a lifetime pass, so I could go up there for free whenever I wanted. Last time I was in New York, I tried to use it, and it turned out it had expired. It wasn't a lifetime pass—it was only good for one year. The guy at the elevator looked at it, and he stopped me. I told him, 'I climbed this building.' He said,

'Oh, okay, you can go up.' I identify with the building. When I heard about the explosion, I thought of doing something—I don't know, writing a letter to the building, to the Port Authority or somebody, expressing my concern and apologies. It was like when a friend gets hurt."

(1993)

BAGS IN TREES

This is the season of plastic bags stuck in trees. Stray shopping bags—many of them white, with handles, perhaps from a deli or a fruit-and-vegetable store originally—roll along the streets, fill with air, levitate like disembodied undershirts, fly, snag by their handles in the branches. Trees wave them in the breeze. They luff and whirr like spinnakers and twist into knots. Daniel, a guy who works at the Brooklyn Botanic Garden, was removing a plastic bag from a Japanese flowering cherry tree at the Eastern Parkway entrance with a leaf rake as I walked by. He held the rake above him at arm's length and snatched at the bag with the tines. It took him a while; finally, he pulled the bag down and squashed it into a ball in his hand. I asked if I could see it. Its blue logo read, "MARTIN PAINT . . . 'It Ain't Just Paint.' "

I walked around Brooklyn looking at plastic bags stuck in trees. I got a sore neck from craning up. I saw yellow Tower Records bags, tan bags, red bags like the kind you get in Chinatown, Key Food bags, C-Town bags. Last season's bags have shredded into a sort of plastic Spanish moss. Big black trash bags become involved in branches in a sprawling and complicated way. Over time, light-colored bags darken and dark ones fade until all are a variety of gray. There is a lot of other stuff in trees, too. Second most common, apparently, is audiocassette tape. It wraps around branches and glistens. Next come balloons, both rubber and silvery-plastic. Next come promotional pennants, the kind used-car lots fly. I also saw:

a catalog from a discount office-supply store in a cypress on Washington Avenue

a jacket with a quilted orange lining, a shredded T-shirt, some string, a wad of newspaper, and a red plastic plant hanger in a pin oak at Sixteenth and Prospect Park West

a white baby bunting with a blue-and-pink design and a drawstring at the bottom hem in a tree on Prospect Park West

a white sash, perhaps from a jujitsu uniform, in a tree on McDonald Avenue (there's a jujitsu place just up the street)

a small black folded umbrella in a tree at Fort Hamilton Parkway and Fifty-sixth Street

an old tire tied to a tree by a blue fitted sheet printed with Disney characters at the corner of Sixty-first Street

a whitewall bicycle tire in a maple at Seventy-first Street

a piece of angle iron, possibly from a bed frame, in an ailanthus by the highway bridge at Seventy-ninth and Seventh

a pair of white Nike high-top sneakers and a pair of high-tops with no visible brand hanging by the laces from a tree at Fifty-ninth Street

thirty-eight pairs of sneakers and other footwear (motorcycle boots, work boots), a pair of dark-red boxing gloves, and a little red-devil doll hanging in a tree at Forty-fifth and Fifth

sneakers, toy guns, teddy bears, and a pair of women's white high-heeled shoes in a big London plane tree on Fifth between Forty-third and Forty-second

a stuffed toy bunny, more women's shoes, more sneakers, a ball of kite string, and a dish drainer in a London plane tree next to that

in a maple above the Prospect Expressway, an unidentifiable wad of leaves and cotton or wool—possibly a nest

(1993)

TO MR. WINSLOW

On June 1, in the afternoon, four teenagers approached a forty-two-year-old drama teacher named Allyn Winslow on Quaker Hill, in Brooklyn's Prospect Park, and tried to steal his new mountain bike. When he resisted and rode away, they shot him four times with a .22-caliber pistol. He rode down the hill to the cobbled path leading to the Picnic House, fell off his bike, and died. The TV news that evening showed the bike on the grass, and his body, covered by a sheet, next to it. I recognized the spot where he lay. I take my daughter to the pond nearby to throw bread to the ducks. She and I had sat there, or near there.

I walked by the spot the next day. It was marked by a wad of discarded surgical tape and an inside-out surgical glove. The day after, when I went by there I saw a Timberland shoe box with a bouquet of flowers in it, and a glass wine carafe with more flowers. In the shoe box was a piece of lined paper on which someone had written in blue ink: "To the biker Mr. Winslow, May you be in a better place with angels on a cloud." These words echoed in the media as reporters quoted and misquoted them. Men and women were carrying microphones and TV cameras in the vicinity, and if you weren't careful they would interview you. About a week later, an American flag had been stuck into the ground next to the shoe box. There was a bunch of papers in a clear plastic envelope, and the one on top said "AVENGE THIS ACT OF COWARDICE." In and around the shoe box were notes addressed to Mr. Winslow and his wife and their two children, a blue-and-white striped ribbon, a ceramic pipe, a bike rider's reflector badge in the image of a peace sign, a red-and-white bandanna, a flyer from the Guardian Angels organization, and an announcement of an upcoming service to be held in his memory.

The following week, the accumulation around the shoe box had grown. The flowers in it and in the wine carafe were fresh—roses, peonies, yellow freesias. Someone had arranged many pinecones and sprigs of oak leaves in a circle on the perimeter. In the ground by the flag was a cross made of wood, bound with red ribbon and draped with a string of purple glass beads, and, near the cross, a photocopy of a newspaper photograph of Allyn Winslow. A Dover edition of Shakespeare's *Complete Sonnets* rested on a pedestal made of a cross section of a branch from a London plane tree. There were also several anti-NRA stickers, a blue candle in a plastic cup, and a five of spades from a pack of Bicycle playing cards. Chunks of paving stones held down a poster showing the number of people killed in 1990 by handguns in various countries: 13 in Sweden, 91 in Switzerland, 87 in Japan, 68 in Canada, 10,567 in the United States. A girl visiting the park on a class picnic asked another girl, "Is he buried here?"

A week or two later, many of the items had vanished. Someone had burned the flag, but the charred flagpole remained. The cross, broken off at the base, lay on the ground. The plastic cup with the candle was cracked. The grass around the spot was worn down in a circle and littered with dried flower stems. The carafe had a big chip out of the top. The shoe box had begun to sag. The papers were gone, except for a rain-stained sign saying, "To Honor, To Mourn Allyn Winslow," and a pamphlet, "Verses of Comfort, Assurance and Salvation."

By mid-July, the shoe box was in pieces. There were a few rocks, two small forked branches stuck in the ground, the ashes of a small fire, and a "You gotta have Park!" button. By mid-August, the tramped-down grass had begun to grow back. I noticed a piece of red-and-white string and a scrap from the shoe box. By September, so little of the memorial remained that the spot was hard to find. A closer look revealed the burned patch, some red-and-white string now faded to pink, and flower stems so scattered and broken you'd have to know what they were to recognize them.

Just now—a bright, chilly fall day—I went by the place again. Color in the park's trees had reached its peak. In a grove of buckskin-brown oaks, yellow shot up the fountain of a ginkgo tree. A flock of pigeons rose all at once and glided to a new part of the Long Meadow, circling once before landing, like a dog before it lies down. A police car slipped around the corner of the Picnic House, a one-man police scooter rode down the path, a police helicopter flew by just above the trees. At first, I could find no trace of the memorial at all: grass and clover have reclaimed the bared dirt. I got down on one knee, muddying my pants. Finally, I found a wooden stake broken off about half an inch above the ground: the base of the memorial cross, probably—the only sign of the unmeasured sorrows that converge here.

(1993)

BAGS IN TREES II

Last year at this time I talked about the phenomenon of plastic bags stuck in trees. I did not mention one fact: I don't like plastic bags stuck in trees. Maybe it was a mistake to notice them in the first place; now I notice them everywhere. The London plane trees on my street in Brooklyn are old for city trees and have grown toward the light and away from the buildings, so that now they lean over the street and nearly meet. In a high branch just across from my window, a cluster of plastic party balloons and ribbons on a stick became lodged in the late 1980s. I watched it go from sort of festive to unrecognizable as it persisted like a debt. Storms that strewed branches all over the street did not budge it. One day, I told my friend Tim about it, and we considered what to do.

At Space Surplus Metals, on Church Street, downtown, we bought one eight-and-a-half-foot and one seven-foot length of stout aluminum tube about an inch across. One length of tube just fit inside the other. Tim is a jeweler, and he took both tubes to his shop and drilled holes in them so they could be held together by a bolt and nut, and he made a device to fit into the other end of the narrower length. This device was a configuration of short, bendable steel rods soldered to a piece of brass pipe. It looked, very roughly, like a hand with crooked and spread fingers, the middle finger longer, upright, and sharpened into a cutting hook. Assembled, the snagger (as we called it) was about sixteen feet long. Tim brought it to my house early one morning, and we put it together. It lacked about two feet of reaching the party balloons. I went back inside and got a kitchen stool. Tim is tall, and he stood on the stool on tiptoe. The hook end of the snagger made contact. A few twists, a few pulls, and the ancient remnants fell to the sidewalk. The tree seemed to shiver like an unsaddled horse.

We walked all over my neighborhood plucking bags. The snagger worked great—a twist of the crooked metal fingers would inveigle the bag, then the sharpened hook would cut it free. In just a few hours, we had removed scores of bags. Old, shredded ones took a lot of monkeying around with, but new, fresh ones sometimes came free in a single motion. The sensation was like having your arm suddenly extended sixteen feet, and the satisfaction like getting something out of your eye. Dangling above traffic makes the bags sooty, and they soon turned our hands a graphite color. A woman passed by, looked at us, and said, "Oh, it's the bag-removal guys." Then she asked us to go to her house and remove some bags from the trees in front. She carefully gave us her address. After she walked on, Tim said, "She doesn't know there *are* no bag-removal guys."

Recently, Tim made another length for the snagger.

Now we can insinuate it more than twenty-five feet through the airy upper realms of ginkgos and lindens and oaks to snatch bags that had eluded us before and had assumed that they had tenure. Last weekend, we were snagging at Collect Pond Park, a bestrewn square plot of pavement and scuffed dirt and benches surrounded by court buildings downtown. Tim's brother, Bill, came, too, and we spelled each other. Holding your arms up that long is tiring. Tim climbed on a "Don't Walk" sign to reach a very high pink plastic bag. We also removed a leather belt, a pair of sneakers, an electrical cord and plug, and some tulle. We spent an hour on a bunch of unidentifiable plastic—a drop cloth, maybe—draping the branches like an exploded fright wig. People stared at us in uneasy incomprehension. The next day, there were nine new bags in two of the trees we had cleaned.

In the Ohio town where I grew up, only the water tower and the church steeples were higher than the trees. Trees occupied the region between us and the sky, and we spent a lot of time looking up into them to see how strong the wind was, or daydreaming. Plastic bags did not get stuck in them, but I did. Once, I climbed an elm in our backyard and wedged my leg between the trunk and a nearly parallel branch. I could not get my arms around the tree to hold on, and so dangled by my leg and yelled. My mother ran to the house being built across the street, and workmen came with a long two-by-four and pried me free.

(1994)

ON THE FLOOR

It gets light early now. The other morning at about five-thirty, I was asleep on the foldout bed in the living room—exiled by my wife for snoring—with the windows open when a strange and loud noise woke me. Asleep, I thought first it was coyotes yipping, or Arab women ululating. When I got up and went to the window, I saw it was two groups of kids of about high-school age shouting at each other across the bright, empty street. Each group was a mix of boys and girls, and the boys and girls alike wore baggy jeans low on their waists, sneakers laced or unlaced, long T-shirts, baggy jackets. The girls wore big gold earrings. Their shouting had an echoey, jangled, scrambled quality. It sounded like a chorus of high-pitched voices shouting the word "mother-fucker" through a blender.

I don't have a regular job, and so I usually ride the subways at hours other than rush hour. Often, in the early morning or in midafternoon, I find myself riding with high-school kids. I eavesdrop on them, which takes slight effort early in the mornings and no effort at all in the afternoons. On their way to school, the kids are kind of subdued, but in the afternoon they are revved up and loud. Once or twice, I have heard conversations about classes; once, some tough-looking boys got on the train and stood by me, and one of them said, "I can't wait until I get my program loaded." But mostly they seem to talk about violence. I have overheard several conversations on the subject of whether it is better to get shot or cut. (Shot wins, no contest; nobody wants to get cut.) Many conversations are about shooting and running. "He come runnin' down the steps shootin'—*pop-pop-pop-pop.*" When I was a kid, guns went *bang*; now they go *pop-pop-pop-pop*. Anyone who is shot or cut ends up layin' on the floor—never the ground. Everything beneath one's feet in the city is now called the floor. "Motherfucker," of course, is a common word, maybe the most common; and the word for "guy," used in a companionable sense, is "nigger," pronounced "nigga." It is adaptable to other races, as in, "Those white niggas be sittin' on the floor smokin' weed." Conversations about, say, wringing blood from a washcloth after a shooting coexist with ordinary talk and pastimes on the subway. I heard a baby-faced boy with long eyelashes say to a girl sitting across the aisle, "Bitch say to me, 'I want you to fuck him up good, shoot the motherfucker.' I went to the motherfucker, I told him straight up, 'Man, your ol' lady says she'd pay me to *do* you, man.' He say to me, 'Man, I really respect you for comin' to tell me like this, I like your style,' " etc. In the next seat, a white woman of about my age and heft was reading, intently, Elliott Roosevelt's *Murder in the Rose Garden.*

I went downstairs and stood on the stoop to watch the kids. They ignored me, barefoot in pajamas, as they moved up the street in no particular order, the smaller group yielding ground to the larger. Occasional phrases would emerge from the stream of their yelling, but mainly the same word was repeated again and again—a frantic, urgent iteration, like the sound of a car engine that won't turn over. I kept looking from one kid to another, trying to judge if any was angry enough to take the dispute to the next level. Their faces, the way they yelled and moved gave no clue. Neighbors more sensible than I had by then called the cops. Police cars pulled up suddenly and stopped in that every-which-way style of theirs. Some of the police talked to one group of kids, some to the other. Three or four kids were put in the backseat of a police car, and it drove away. The remaining kids dispersed. I went inside and, in a few minutes, came out again. Four or five of the kids had been sitting on our stoop. They got up and walked slowly back down the street in the direction they had come from. Two of the boys had their arms draped around girls' shoulders. I recognized the posture: it was the wrung-out, let-down, dishrag limpness that comes after an explosion of adrenaline when the danger has gone. Their baggy clothes exaggerated the look even more. Only then did I realize how scared the kids had been, and that they had understood all along that they were risking their lives. Nothing in their words—in their single, repeated, almost meaningless word—had conveyed their fear to me. I don't remember ever being that scared as a kid. Most people get that scared only a few times in their lives. My downstairs neighbor came out the door on his way to the gym. A woman several doors down emerged with her twin miniature collies. Under the new leaves at the end of the block, the kids were almost out of sight.

(1994)

SUMMER RULES

There are dozens and dozens of playgrounds in Brooklyn. Most are paved with worn asphalt stained by faded graffiti and oil spills and chocolate splotches and white dots of chewing gum. Trash collects in the corners of some, and starlings police it. At many playgrounds, the bathrooms are closed. The drinking fountains, when working, have shreds of burst water balloons in the basins, which are of a concrete so old and water marked as to seem hardly man-made. Trees shade some playgrounds, but others lie open to the sun. Officially, many playgrounds have names like Monsignor McGolrick Park or Betty K. Rappaport Playground or Joe Galapo Playground or Bill Brown Park. Unofficially, a few parks commemorate, in large graffiti paintings on the walls of handball courts, people like Imel (November 20, 1967–August 20, 1993) or Cliff (July 25, 1947–January 14, 1993: "Rest in Peace, Daddy!"). In any playground, you hear the sound of balls bouncing. No playground is so forlorn that it doesn't have four or six guys shooting a game of listless hot-weather hoops.

Some playgrounds are jumping. On a weekend afternoon at Nostrand Playground, in Flatbush, young guys in wheelchairs do small stunts by the gate and shout greetings to passersby. Venders sell sugarcane and mango halves and split green coconuts. When a person gets up from a bench, someone soon takes his place. Candy-colored cars at the curb give off a cicada-throb of music. Kids swing so high on the swings that the chains become slack; they flop on their stomachs, and their hair grazes the ground. A guy holding a twenty-two-ounce bottle of St. Ides malt liquor in one hand and a slipping-around girl on Rollerblades in the other says, "Look up! Stop lookin' down!" Overhead, an unfrayed American flag flies straight out in the breeze.

At Paerdegat Park, some blocks away, men play dominoes and drink malta from small brown bottles. They exclaim as they slap the smooth tiles down hard. One man wears a T-shirt decorated with pictures of the members of the Trinidad and Tobago soccer team, a World Cup qualifier in 1990. Suddenly there is a bang, a screech of brakes, a scary, violent vibration from the street alongside. All the people look in that direction, like a herd of deer. A teenage boy lies on the pavement. He doesn't cry; he is moving one leg back and forth. Someone puts a knapsack under his head. A short, bald brown man—the driver who hit him?— stands over him with pencil and notebook, explaining to bystanders with a repeated gesture of his hand. A man from the crowd begins to direct traffic; on the man's T-shirt is a black-

and-white picture taken from the videotape of the police beating Rodney King. An EMS truck arrives, and two paramedics get out and pull on latex gloves. The paramedics lean over the boy, they strap immobilizing supports to his head and leg and neck, they put him on a stretcher, they lift the stretcher into the back of the truck. The boy stares upward, his eyes blinking, his skin the color of clay.

At Albemarle Playground, in Borough Park, the buildings and trees all around make the half block of space seem taller than it is wide. Gray-haired ladies wearing new black Adidas with white stripes play cards, and boys in yarmulkes shoot high-powered squirt guns at girls in skirts down to their shins. Black and Asian and Hispanic and white boys play a fast game of basketball, in which it seems that everybody gets a shot. Four shirtless white guys are playing handball, towels draped around their necks. A dark-eyed, downcast little boy wearing a Rangers T-shirt hanging to his knees walks onto the handball court. With him are a frizzy-haired woman and a thickset man whose upwardly tapering haircut makes him look like a wedge. The man talks to the handball players, waving his finger in their faces. The woman says they took the boy's ball and made him beg for it back. The handball players hold their palms up in conciliation. Pointing, the wedge-shaped man tells the handball players, "This is my son!" Then he walks to the middle of the playground and sets his feet apart and says, "Listen, everybody. Alvaro is my son! Do you all hear that? Alvaro is: *My. Son.* If you disrespect him, I'm gonna fuck you up! If I can't fight you, I'll bite your dick off! Either you swallow my dick or I'll swallow yours!" Still talking, he walks from the playground, then trots away down Twelfth Avenue. The boy and the frizzy-haired woman leave. The gray-haired women in the Adidas return to their card game. The basketball again begins to bounce.

(1994)

STREET SCENE

On a Saturday morning I left my Brooklyn apartment to shop for a dinner party and saw a crowd—baseball caps, legs straddling bicycles, an arm holding a lamp stand with a dangling price tag—around a person on the sidewalk. I was almost at my doorstep; I went closer and saw a woman lying on her back with her lips turned into her mouth and her eyes neither open nor closed. Her hair was gray, her face the same color as the pavement. A slight brown-haired woman was giving her mouth-to-mouth resuscitation, while a well-built brown-skinned man with hair close cropped like a skullcap was performing chest massage. He and the woman giving mouth-to-mouth were counting. "One, two, three, four, *five.*" Then he would pause and she would breathe into the woman's mouth.

A police car drove up and a young Hispanic cop got out. He went over to the woman and talked to the pair trying to revive her. Someone pointed out to him the woman's son, a tall, gangly man who stood nearby, kind of bobbing up and down and nodding to himself. The cop patted the son on the arm and spoke to him. A large, lumpy-faced man with his pants high on his waist said to me, "The ambulance will never come. They never come when you call anymore. They don't care. In New York nobody cares. People are so arrogant on the street in Manhattan. I call New York a lost city. Used to be a great city, now it's a lost city. People are nicer out west or upstate. I went to Methodist Hospital and the nurse wouldn't talk to me. I told her right to her face . . ." After a minute I realized it made no difference if I listened to him or not. The pair at work on the woman paused for a moment while the man asked if anyone had a razor so he could cut the woman's shirt. Someone found a pocket knife. He bent over his work again. Minutes passed. The cop asked if he was getting tired and he said he wasn't. Sirens rose in the distance, faded. Then one rose and didn't fade, and in the next second an Emergency Medical Service truck from Long Island College Hospital pulled up. The chest-massage guy didn't quit until the EMS paramedic took over; then he straightened up, looked at the truck, and said, "Long *Island*? Fuckin' Methodist is only three blocks away."

The EMS guys put the woman on a stretcher and lifted her into the back of the truck. Hands gathered up a few items the woman had dropped on the sidewalk; someone pointed out her false teeth. The woman who had been giving mouth-to-mouth bent over and picked up the teeth. She paused just a second before touching them. I thought this was from squeamishness; then I saw it was from care. Gently she handed the teeth to one of the paramedics. Then she and the chest-massage guy parted without a word, or none that I saw. The guy walked toward his car, a two-tone Pontiac. Apparently he

82

had just been driving by; its door was still open. I went up to him and thanked him for what he had done. I shook his hand. His strength went right up my arm like a warm current. I ran after the woman, who was now well down the block. I tapped her shoulder and she turned and I said thank you. Her eyes were full of what had just happened. There were tears on her upper cheeks. She said something like, "Oh, of course, don't mention it." She was a thin-faced white woman with Prince Valiant hair and a green windbreaker—an ordinary-looking person, but glowingly beautiful.

The EMS guys and the cop worked on the woman in the back of the truck with the doors open. The crowd dispersed. The son crouched inside the truck holding the IV bottle for a while; then he stood outside again. Eventually the cop got out of the back of the truck. The son climbed in, the EMS guys closed the doors, and the truck drove off with sirens going. The cop sat in his car. The window was down. I walked over and asked, "Excuse me—did they ever get a pulse?" He winced slightly at the nakedness of my question. A pause. Then he shook his head. "Nahhh. Not really."

I went to the park across the street. A bunch of kids were hanging around the entrance jawing back and forth at each other. In my neighborhood there is a gang called NAB, or Ninth Avenue Boys. Newspaper stories say they've done a lot of beatings and robberies nearby. From a few feet away I heard one kid say to another, "You shut your stupid fuckin' chicken-breath mouth." I felt as strong as the strangers I had just talked to. I walked through the kids without fear.

(1995)

IN THE STACKS

The main reading room of Butler Library, at Columbia University, is long and high ceilinged. On a Saturday afternoon in summer, eight widely scattered people are studying in it. All appear to be of Asian descent; five are women. The tall windows are open; fans on tall stands push the hot air around. People and a dog are playing with a Frisbee on the lawn somewhere under the windows. You can hear the dog's jaws when he makes a catch. From the tables in the periodicals room, down the hall, you can see across a tennis court into the windows of a dormitory. A woman sits at a window, holding her long hair up off her neck with one hand.

Butler has twelve floors of library stacks—some aboveground, some partly below. The main entrance to the stacks, near the checkout desk, is through a propped-open door with a worn marble lintel. A librarian on a stool used to preside there sometimes, like a border guard. Past the entry, the dimensions narrow to submarine scale. Light in the stacks is dim, from overhead fluorescent bulbs. The central aisles in the acres of floor-to-ceiling bookshelves remain lit, but each tributary aisle is dark until you light it with an individual switch that is also a timer. If you turn the switch full to the right, the light in the aisle will stay on for fifteen minutes. Sometimes I turn the switch, go down the aisle, find the book I want, become engrossed, sit on the floor; then there's a click, and I'm in the dark. I sit in the dark for a while. At this same moment, Amsterdam Avenue is jumping, the trains to the Hamptons are packed, Washington Square is a hive. On certain summer days, the stacks of Butler are as quiet and lonesome as any place in the city.

At wider places in the aisles are chairs and wooden study tables big enough for only one person. I choose a table and read, say, a travel narrative from the nineteenth century, which crackles when it's opened and gives off hundred-year-old dust. Always, my eye starts to wander, tugged away by the graffiti on the table: "All men are meat"; "CIA killed Disney"; "BΘΠ dominates campus social life." In the remote parts of Butler, some tables are not just written on but embossed, washed, blued with spidery graffiti. I have found graffiti protesting wars from the Gulf War all the way back to the Korean. Only the more recent entries are really readable; to read the faded-out, historic ones you must get at an angle to the table and let the marks the pens made in the wood catch the light: "⊕ Ban the Bomb"; "IMPEACH NI✦ON"; "Mondale Is Mush."

In the silence, the graffiti is a cacophony: "DAVID BOWIE IS SUPREME—GOD IS SUPREME—THEREFORE DAVID BOWIE IS GOD."

"You should be shot you fucking ASSHOLE!"

"They say that man is wise and I believe them—but then I also once believed in love."

"Oh go fuck yourself. Be wistful somewhere else."

"ΒΘΠ JOCKS RULE."

"Beta Theta Pi is full of idiots who think they're men because they can play speed-quarters until they puke. I love it when a 'man' vomits. (Trust me, I was there.)"

"I cut myself last night with a razor because I need help."

"YIDDISH FOREVER YOUNG."

"*Das ist nicht Richtig.*"

"Frat Neanderthal!"

"Bullshit stereotype you bigot! Liberal!"

"Gentlemen do be kind enough with the harsh words."

"Read LEVITICUS."

"Blacks are the *real* racists."

"We only learn from people like you."

". . . And Al Sharpton!"

"Stop acting like martyrs and start treating whites like real people."

"Face reality—you are just frightened by the concept that people of color are educating themselves in white man's institutions (i.e. Columbia) and will one day step not on the white race but on *you*."

"TOMORROW THERE IS A PHYSICS EXAM (11/15/83) HELP!"

Mostly, the graffiti is about longing. Libraries generate longing. It collects in the shelves and rustles under the desks and zaps people like static electricity. At Butler, the character of the longing is mostly male. More women should write on these desks, to improve the mix. Guys write, "Mary P. I'm in total love with you" and "There's this beautiful girl sitting in front of me; I cannot study," and they ask specific women for dates, and they say, "I want to make love to you in the stacks," and they describe acts they say they've committed on these very tables, and they say, "When Cara B—— struts through these dusty aisles this ancient storeroom of treasures comes to life," and they say that the best reason to go to Columbia is a certain woman named So-and-So, and they expound on amatory things they did or do. A woman's hand responds, "*You wish.*"

(1995)

TAKE THE F

Brooklyn, New York, has the undefined, hard-to-remember shape of a stain. I never know what to tell people when they ask me where in it I live. It sits at the western tip of Long Island at a diagonal that does not conform neatly to the points of the compass. People in Brooklyn do not describe where they live in terms of north or west or south. They refer instead to their neighborhoods and to the nearest subway lines. I live on the edge of Park Slope, a neighborhood by the crest of a low ridge that runs through the borough. Prospect Park is across the street. Airplanes in the landing pattern for LaGuardia Airport sometimes fly right over my building; every few minutes, on certain sunny days, perfectly detailed airplane shadows slide down my building and up the building opposite in a blink. You can see my building from the plane—it's on the left-hand side of Prospect Park, the longer patch of green you cross after the expanse of Green-Wood Cemetery.

We moved to a co-op apartment in a four-story building a week before our daughter was born. She is now six. I grew up in the country and would not have expected ever to live in Brooklyn. My daughter is a city kid, with less sympathy for certain other parts of the country. When we visited Montana, she was disappointed by the scarcity of pizza places. I overheard her explaining—she was three or four then—to a Montana kid about Brooklyn. She said, "In Brooklyn, there is a lot of broken glass, so you have to wear shoes. And, there is good pizza." She is stern in her judgment of pizza. At the very low end of the pizza-ranking scale is some pizza she once had in New Hampshire, a category now called New Hampshire pizza. In the middle is some okay pizza she once had at the Bronx Zoo, which she calls zoo pizza. At the very top is the pizza at the pizza place where the big kids go, about two blocks from our house.

Our subway is the F train. It runs under our building and shakes the floor. The F is generally a reliable train, but one spring as I walked in the park I saw emergency vehicles gathered by a concrete-sheathed hole in the lawn. Firemen lifted a metal lid from the hole and descended into it. After a while, they reappeared, followed by a few people, then dozens of people, then a whole lot of people—passengers from a disabled F train, climbing one at a time out an exit shaft. On the F, I sometimes see large women in straw hats reading a newspaper called the *Caribbean Sunrise*, and Orthodox Jews bent over Talmudic texts in which the footnotes have footnotes, and groups of teenagers wearing identical red bandannas with identical red plastic baby pacifiers in the corners of their mouths, and female couples in porkpie hats, and young men with the silhouettes of the Manhattan skyline razored into their short side hair from one temple around to the other, and Russian-speaking men with thick wrists and big wristwatches, and a hefty, tall woman with long, straight blond hair who hums and closes her eyes and absently practices cello fingerings on the metal subway pole. As I watched the F train passengers emerge among the grass and trees of Prospect Park, the faces were as varied as usual, but the expressions of indignant surprise were all about the same.

Just past my stop, Seventh Avenue, Manhattan-bound F trains rise from underground to cross the Gowanus Canal. The train sounds different—lighter, quieter—in the open air. From the elevated tracks, you can see the roofs of many houses stretching back up the hill to Park Slope, and a bumper crop of rooftop graffiti, and neon signs for Eagle Clothes and Kentile Floors, and flat expanses of factory roofs where seagulls stand on one leg around puddles in the sagging spots. There are fuel-storage tanks surrounded by earthen barriers, and slag piles, and conveyor belts leading down to the oil-slicked waters of the canal. On certain days, the sludge at the bottom of the canal causes it to bubble. Two men fleeing the police jumped in the canal a while ago; one made it across, the other quickly died. When the subway doors open at the Smith–Ninth Street stop, you can see the bay and sometimes smell the ocean breeze. This stretch of elevated is the highest point of the New York subway system. To the south you can see the Verrazano-Narrows Bridge, to the north the World Trade towers. For just a few moments, the Statue of Liberty appears between passing buildings. Pieces of a neighborhood—laundry on clotheslines, a standup swimming pool, a plaster saint, a satellite dish, a rectangle of lawn—slide by like quickly dealt cards. Then the train descends again; growing over the wall just before the tunnel is a wisteria bush, which blooms pale blue every May.

I have spent days, weeks on the F train. The trip from Seventh Avenue to midtown Manhattan is long enough so that every ride can produce its own minisociety of riders, its own forty-minute Ship of Fools. Once a woman an arm's length from me on a crowded train pulled a knife on a man who threatened her. I remember the argument and the principals, but mostly I remember the knife—its flat, curved wood-grain handle inlaid with brass fittings at each end, its long, tapered blade. Once a man sang the words of the Lord's Prayer to a mournful, syncopated tune, and he fitted the mood of the morning so exactly that when he asked for money at the end the riders reached for their wallets and purses as if he'd pulled a gun. Once a big white kid with some friends was teasing a small old Hispanic lady, and when he got off the train I looked at him through the window and he slugged it hard next to my face. Once a thin woman and a fat woman sitting side by side had a long and loud conversation about someone they intended to slap silly: "Her butt be in the *hospital*!" "Bring out the ar-*tillery*!" The terminus of the F in Brooklyn is at Coney Island, not far from the beach. At an off hour, I boarded the train and found two or three passengers and, walking around on the floor, a crab. The passengers were looking at the crab. Its legs clicked on the floor like varnished fingernails. It moved in this direction, then that, trying to get comfortable. It backed itself under a seat, against the wall. Then it scooted out just after some new passengers had sat down there, and they really screamed. Passengers at the next stop saw it and laughed. When a boy lifted his foot as if to stomp it, everybody cried, "Noooh!" By the time we reached Jay Street–Borough Hall, there were maybe a dozen of us in the car, all absorbed in watching the crab. The car doors opened and a heavyset woman with good posture entered. She looked at the crab; then, sternly, at all of us. She let a moment pass. Then she demanded, "*Whose* is *that?*" A few stops later, a short man with a mustache took a manila envelope, bent down, scooped the crab into it, closed it, and put it in his coat pocket.

The smells in Brooklyn: coffee, fingernail polish, eucalyptus, the breath from laundry rooms, pot roast, Tater Tots. A woman I know who grew up here says she moved away because she could not stand the smell of cooking food in the hallway of her parents' building. I feel just the opposite. I used to live in a converted factory above an army-navy store, and I like being in a place that smells like people live there. In the mornings, I sometimes wake to the smell of toast, and I still don't know exactly whose toast it is. And I prefer living in a borough of two and a half million inhabitants, the most of any borough in the city. I think of all the rural places, the pine-timbered canyons and within-commuting-distance farmland, that we are preserving by not living there. I like the immensities of the borough, the unrolling miles of Eastern Parkway and Ocean Parkway and Linden Boulevard, and the disheveled outlying parks strewn with tree limbs and with shards of glass held together by liquor bottle labels, and the tough bridges—the Williamsburg and the Manhattan— and the gentle Brooklyn Bridge. And I like the way the people talk; some really do have Brooklyn accents, really do say "dese" and "dose." A week or two ago, a group of neighbors stood on a street corner watching a peregrine falcon on a building cornice contentedly eating a pigeon it had caught, and the sunlight came through its tail feathers, and a woman said to a man, "Look at the tail, it's so ah-range," and the man replied, "Yeah, I soar it." Like many Americans, I fear living in a nowhere, in a place that is no-place; in Brooklyn, that doesn't trouble me at all.

Everybody, it seems, is here. At Grand Army Plaza, I have seen traffic tie-ups caused by Haitians and others rallying in support of President Aristide, and by St. Patrick's Day parades, and by Jews of the Lubavitcher sect celebrating the birthday of their Grand Rebbe with a slow procession of ninety-three motor homes—one for each year of his life. Local taxis have bumper stickers that say "Allah Is Great"; one of the men who made the bomb that blew up the World Trade Center used an apartment just a few blocks from me. When an election is held in Russia, crowds line up to cast ballots at a Russian polling place in Brighton Beach. A while ago, I volunteer-taught reading at a public elementary school across the park. One of my students, a girl, was part Puerto Rican, part Greek, and part Welsh. Her looks were a lively combination, set off by sea-green eyes. I went to a map store in Manhattan and bought maps of Puerto Rico, Greece, and Wales to read with her, but they didn't interest her. A teacher at the school was directing a group of students to set up chairs for a program in the auditorium, and she said to me, "We have a problem here—each of these kids speaks a different language." She asked the kids to tell me where they were from. One was from Korea, one from

Brazil, one from Poland, one from Guyana, one from Tai-
wan. In the program that followed, a chorus of fourth and
fifth graders sang "God Bless America," "You're a Grand
Old Flag," and "I'm a Yankee-Doodle Dandy."

People in my neighborhood are mostly white, and middle class or above. People in neighborhoods nearby are
mostly not white, and mostly middle class or below. Everybody uses Prospect Park. On summer days, the park teems
with sound—the high note is kids screaming in the water
sprinklers at the playground, the midrange is radios and tape
players, and the bass is idling or speeding cars. People bring
lawn furniture and badminton nets and coolers, and then
they barbecue. Charcoal smoke drifts into the neighborhood.
Last year, local residents upset about the noise and litter and
smoke began a campaign to outlaw barbecuing in the park.
There was much unfavorable comment about "the barbecuers." Since most of the barbecuers, as it happens, are black
or Hispanic, the phrase "Barbecuers Go Home," which someone spray-painted on the asphalt at the Ninth Street entrance to the park, took on a pointed, unkind meaning. But
then park officials set up special areas for barbecuing, and the
barbecuers complied, and the controversy died down.

Right nearby is a shelter for homeless people. Sometimes
people sleep on the benches along the park, sometimes they
sleep in the foyer of our building. Once I went downstairs,
my heart pounding, to evict a homeless person who I had
been told was there. The immediate, unquestioning way she
left made me feel bad; later I always said "Hi" to her and
gave her a dollar when I ran into her. One night, late, I saw
her on the street, and I asked her her last name (by then I al-

ready knew her first name) and for a moment she couldn't recall it. At this, she shook her head in mild disbelief.

There's a guy I see on a bench along Prospect Park West all the time. Once I walked by carrying my year-old son, and the man said, "Someday he be carrying you." At the local copy shop one afternoon, a crowd was waiting for copies and faxes when a man in a houndstooth fedora came in seeking signatures for a petition to have the homeless shelter shut down. To my surprise, and his, the people in the copy shop instantly turned on him. "I suppose because they're poor they shouldn't even have a place to sleep at night," a woman said as he backed out the door. On the park wall across the street from my building, someone has written in black marker:

COPS PROTECT CITIZENS
WHO PROTECT US FROM COPS.

Sometimes I walk from my building downhill and north, along the Brooklyn waterfront, where cargo ships with scuffed sides and prognathous bows lean overhead. Sometimes I walk by the Brooklyn Navy Yard, its docks now too dormant to attract saboteurs, its long expanses of chain-link fence tangled here and there with the branches of ailanthus trees growing through. Sometimes I head southwest, keeping more or less to the high ground—Bay Ridge—along Fifth Avenue, through Hispanic neighborhoods that stretch in either direction as far as you can see, and then through block after block of Irish. I follow the ridge to its steep descent to the water at the Verrazano Narrows; Fort Hamilton,

an army post dating from 1814, is there, and a small Episcopal church called the Church of the Generals. Robert E. Lee
once served as a vestryman of this church, and Stonewall
Jackson was baptized here. Today the church is in the shade
of a forest of high concrete columns supporting an access
ramp to the Verrazano-Narrows Bridge.

Sometimes I walk due south, all the way out Coney Island Avenue. In that direction, as you approach the ocean,
the sky gets bigger and brighter, and the buildings seem to
flatten beneath it. Dry cleaners advertise "Tallis Cleaned
Free with Every Purchase Over Fifteen Dollars." Then you
start to see occasional lines of graffiti written in Cyrillic.
Just past a Cropsey Avenue billboard welcoming visitors to
Coney Island is a bridge over a creek filled nearly to the surface with metal shopping carts that people have tossed there
over the years. A little farther on, the streets open onto the
beach. On a winter afternoon, bundled-up women sit on
the boardwalk on folding chairs around a portable record
player outside a restaurant called Gastronom Moscow. The
acres of trash-dotted sand are almost empty. A bottle of Peter
the Great vodka lies on its side, drops of water from its
mouth making a small depression in the sand. A man with
trousers rolled up to his shins moves along the beach, chop-
ping at driftwood with an axe. Another passerby says, "He's
vorking hard, that guy!" The sunset unrolls light along the
storefronts like tape. From the far distance, little holes in the
sand at the water's edge mark the approach of a short man
wearing hip boots and earphones and carrying a long-
handled metal detector. Treasure hunters dream of the jewelry that people must have lost here over the years. Some say

that this is the richest treasure beach in the Northeast. The man stops, runs the metal detector again over a spot, digs with a clamming shovel, lifts some sand, brushes through it with a gloved thumb, discards it. He goes on, leaving a trail of holes behind him.

I like to find things myself, and I always try to keep one eye on the ground as I walk. So far I have found seven dollars (a five and two ones), an earring in the shape of a strawberry, several personal notes, a matchbook with a 900 number to call to hear "prison sex fantasies," and two spent .25-caliber shells. Once on Carroll Street, I saw a page of text on the sidewalk, and I bent over to read it. It was page 191 from a copy of *Anna Karenina*. I read the whole page. It described Vronsky leaving a gathering and riding off in a carriage. In a great book, the least fragment is great. I looked up and saw a woman regarding me closely from a few feet away. "You're reading," she said wonderingly. "From a distance, I t'ought you were watchin' ants."

My favorite place to walk is the Brooklyn Botanic Garden, not more than fifteen minutes away. It's the first place I take out-of-towners, who may not associate Brooklyn with flowers. In the winter, the garden is drab as pocket lint, and you can practically see all the way through from Flatbush Avenue to Washington Avenue. But then in February or March a few flowerings begin, the snowdrops and the crocuses, and then the yellow of the daffodils climbs Daffodil Hill, and then the magnolias—star magnolias, umbrella magnolias, saucer magnolias—go off all at once, and walking among them is like flying through cumulus clouds. Then the cherry trees blossom, some a soft and glossy red like makeup, others pink as a dessert, and crowds fill the paths on weekends and stand in front of the blossoms in their best clothes and have their pictures taken. Security guards tell people, "No eating, no sitting on the grass—this is a garden, not a park." There are traffic jams of strollers and kids running loose. One security guard jokes into his radio, "There's a pterodactyl on the overlook!" In the pond in the Japanese Garden, ducks lobby for pieces of bread. A duck quacks, in Brooklynese, "Yeah, yeah, yeah," having heard it all before.

Then the cherry blossoms fall, they turn some paths completely pink next to the grass's green, and the petals dry, and people tread them into a fine pink powder. Kids visit on end-of-school-year field trips, and teachers yell, "Shawon, get back on line!" and boys with long T-shirts printed from neck to knee with an image of Martin Luther King's face run by laughing and swatting at one another. The yellow boxes that photographic film comes in fall on the ground, and here and there an empty bag of Crazy Calypso potato chips. The lilacs bloom, each bush with a scent slightly different from the next, and yellow tulips fill big round planters with color so bright it ascends in a column, like a searchlight beam. The roses open on the trellises in the Rose Garden and attract a lively air traffic of bees, and June wedding parties, brides and grooms and their subsidiaries, adjust themselves minutely for photographers there. A rose called the Royal Gold smells like a new bathing suit and is as yellow.

In our building of nine apartments, two people have died and six have been born since we moved in. I like our neighbors—a guy who works for Off-Track Betting, a guy who works for the Department of Correction, a woman who works for Dean Witter, an in-flight steward, a salesperson of subsidiary rights at a publishing house, a restaurant manager, two lawyers, a retired machinist, a Lebanese-born woman of ninety-five—as well as any I've ever had. We keep track of the bigger events in the building with the help of Chris, our downstairs neighbor. Chris lives on the ground floor and often has conversations in the hall while her foot props her door open. When our kids are sick, she brings them her kids' videos to watch, and when it rains she gives us rides to school. One year, Chris became pregnant and had to take a blood-thinning medicine and was in and out of the hospital. Finally, she had a healthy baby and came home, but then began to bleed and didn't stop. Her husband brought the baby to us about midnight and took Chris to the nearest emergency room. Early the next morning, the grandmother came and took the baby. Then for two days nobody heard anything. When we knocked on Chris's door we got no answer and when we called we got an answering machine. The whole building was expectant, spooky, quiet. The next morning I left the house and there in the foyer was Chris. She held her husband's arm, and she looked pale, but she was returning from the hospital under her own steam. I hugged her at the door, and it was the whole building hugging her. I walked to the garden seeing glory everywhere. I went to the Rose Garden and took a big Betsy McCall rose to my face and breathed into it as if it were an oxygen mask.

(1995)

ALL THAT GLITTER

Do you have a problem with glitter? I do. By glitter I mean, of course, the shiny particulate substance used by children in art projects. It is viral. It gets onto surfaces and into niches in your house or apartment, and then it is pretty much there to stay. If you have young kids, chances are there is a piece of glitter within sight of where you are sitting now. And if it turns out the little shiny thing you thought was a piece of glitter was just an illusion, that only strengthens my point: glitter is extra-pernicious because when you know you have it, you see it even in places it isn't. Just to be sure this glitter problem wasn't only mine, I asked around among some people I know:

Elizabeth W., Brooklyn: My son Colin constantly had glitter on his head for the first eighteen months of his life. All second children have a problem with glitter. I now discourage my older son from projects involving glitter. We have a sort of glitter moratorium at our house.

Maggie H., Brooklyn: I see it shining on the children's scalps through their hair. Eyelids are a favorite glitter nesting ground. To scrape it off, you practically have to draw blood. I come home sometimes and look in the mirror and find it on me. I think there should be a greeting card that says, "Sorry I had lunch with you with glitter on my nose."

John H., Queens: We have had glitter parties that were something to behold. Our loft has uneven floorboards, and at night the lines between the boards are a vista of glitter highlights. In our loft it blows into glitter drifts and glitter dunes.

Anne Q., Cambridge, Mass.: Andrew likes to roll tooth-brushes on the floor, and all our toothbrushes have glitter on them. We often have glitter on our food.

Katherine F., Lincoln, Neb.: My God, did you get some on you when you were here? Not long ago, in the craft area in our basement, a can of mixed-color glitter fell on the floor, and one of the cats got in it and then she rolled around in the laundry, and soon afterward we began to notice that we were all glittering.

Amy L., San Francisco: We made a batch of fifty-two glitter valentines for my daughter to send on Valentine's Day, and later I felt so guilty thinking of all that glitter all over everybody's house in San Francisco. My husband Mike is a really, really orderly guy, and as he was Dustbusting it from between the cracks in the floor he looked up at me and said, "Never, ever do this again."

There's a piece of glitter on the carpet between my feet. From here, as I move my head, it flashes like a mirror signal from a distant ridge. Now I lie on the floor and look at it close up, through a photographer's loupe. The carpet strands are a glossy thicket, with the piece of glitter among the branches in the understory. Magnified, it is a coppery gold of uneven sheen. Using a pin and my fingernail, I put it on a page of a magazine. It fills almost exactly the space inside an "n." Seen through the loupe against the flat white of the page, it is a rectangle with a shallow right-angled notch in one corner, which causes it to sort of resemble the profile of Utah. On the arm of my chair is another piece of gold glitter, and I place it on the page, next to the first. Through the loupe, the two are identical, down to the notch in the corner. Elsewhere, I find more glitter, silver colored, not uniform in size, but each piece a precise rectangle. I call a glitter manufacturer and talk to a vice president named Marty. He tells me that glitter is made from rolls of very thin acetate by loud, custom-built glitter-grinding machines. His machines make about a ton of glitter every week.

Ever since the highway department began adding crushed-up bottles to its asphalt mix, certain New York City streets have glittered. Many city curbs and sidewalks glitter with shattered car window that escapes the street sweeper or works its way into the spaces between paving stones. The worn lawns of the park by my house glitter in spots with discarded tiny metal stuff like pop-tops and bottle caps ignored by cleanup crews after bigger prey. In summer, especially in the city, you are surrounded by countless winking shards of light. Just now, my sister-in-law brought over her new baby daughter. I had never seen the baby before, and the baby had never seen New York. Her wide, dark eyes did not seem to blink as she moved them with a series of short adjustments from one new apparition to the next. She is a first child, cared for with the precision parents often give to their first. I looked her over carefully but could find no glitter at all. Before long, a piece will adhere to her, marking her as our own.

(1995)

SOMEPLACE IN QUEENS

Off and on, I get a thing for walking in Queens. One morning, I strayed into that borough from my more usual routes in Brooklyn, and I just kept rambling. I think what drew me on was the phrase "someplace in Queens." This phrase is often used by people who live in Manhattan to describe a Queens location. They don't say the location is simply "in Queens"; they say it is "someplace in Queens," or "in Queens someplace": "All the records are stored in a warehouse someplace in Queens," "His ex-wife lives in Queens someplace." The swooning, overwhelmed quality that the word "someplace" gives to such descriptions is no doubt a result of the fact that people who don't live in Queens see it mostly from the windows of airplanes landing there, at LaGuardia or Kennedy airports. They look out at the mile after mile of apparently identical row houses coming up at them and swoon back in their seats at the unknowability of it all. When I find myself among those houses, with their weight-lifting trophies or floral displays in the front windows, with their green lawns and nasturtium borders and rosebushes and sidewalks stained blotchy purple by crushed berries from the overhanging mulberry trees, and a scent of curry is in the air, and a plane roars above so close I think I could almost recognize someone at a window, I am happy to be someplace in Queens.

Queens is shaped sort of like a brain. The top, or northern border, is furrowed with bays and coves and salt marshes and creeks extending inland from the East River and Long Island Sound. To the west, its frontal lobe adjoins the roughly diagonal line running southeast that separates it from Brooklyn. At its stem is the large, solid mass of Kennedy Airport, at its east the mostly flat back part that borders Nassau County, Long Island. To the south stretches the long, narrow peninsula of Rockaway Beach, which does not really fit my analogy. Queens is the largest New York City borough. It has the longest and widest avenues, the most freeways, and the most crowded subway stations. It has more ethnic groups and nationalities than any other borough; observers say that it has more ethnic diversity than any other place its size on earth. Some of its schools are the city's most overcrowded. In one Queens school district, a dozen or more new pupils enroll every week during the school year, many speaking little English. Classes meet in bathrooms and on stairways; kids use stairs as desks when they practice their spelling, and teachers go home hoarse every night from trying to make themselves heard. Immigrants open stores along the avenues beneath the elevated-train tracks in Queens, the way they used to under the old Second Avenue El on the Lower East Side. Queens has more miles of elevated tracks than any borough, and the streets below them teem.

I like to walk under the elevated tracks early on summer mornings, before people are up. At six-thirty, a steeply pitched shaft of sunlight falls between each pair of dark iron pillars. On down the avenue you see the shafts of light, each tinted with haze, receding after each other into the distance. Sun here is secondary, like sun in a forest or on a reef. Some of the shadows of the El on the empty pavement are solid blocks, some are sun-and-shadow plaid. Traffic lights overhang the intersections from the El's beams and run through their cycles at this hour for no one. Security gates on all the stores are down. There's a sharp tapping as an Asian man turns a corner hitting the top of a fresh pack of cigarettes against his palm. He tears off the cellophane, throws it on the ground, opens the pack, hurries up the steps to the station. Each metallic footstep is distinct. When the noise of the train comes, it's a ringing, clattering pounding that fills this space like a rioting throng. The sound pulses as if the train were bouncing on its rails, and, in fact, if you stand in the station, the floor does seem to trampoline slightly beneath your feet. Then there's the hiss of the air brakes, a moment of quiet, the two notes of the signal for the closing doors, and the racket begins again. In the world under the El, speech-drowning noise comes and goes every few minutes.

Queens specializes in neighborhoods that nonresidents have heard of but could never place on a map. Long Island City, for example, is not someplace out on Long Island but on Queens's East River side, across from midtown Manhattan. High-society families had estates there when that side of the river was New York's Gold Coast. Today, it is Con Ed property, warehouses, and movie-equipment supply places.

You can buy a used police car there for a third off the book price. Astoria is near LaGuardia Airport, just across the river from Rikers Island, which is in the Bronx. Sunnyside is southeast of Long Island City, and below Sunnyside is Maspeth, and below Maspeth is Ridgewood, one of the most solidly blue-collar neighborhoods in the city. Springfield Gardens, in southeast Queens, has many wood-frame houses, and that general area has the city's highest fire-fatality rate. Queens used to be the city's vegetable garden and orchard, and in certain places the old farmland still bulges through the borough's concrete lacings. In Fresh Meadows, in the east middle of the borough, a cherry tree survives that was planted in about 1790. It stands on a small triangular relic of field now strewn with Chinese-restaurant flyers and abutted by the back of a beverage store, a row of small businesses, and some row houses. This year, the tree bore a crop of cherries, just as it did when it was out in the country and Lincoln was a boy.

In Forest Hills, in the middle of the borough, flight attendants in blue uniforms with red scarves wheel suitcase caddies up its sloping sidewalks. Woodside, on the northwest border, is the city's most integrated neighborhood. St. Albans and Cambria Heights, on the east of the borough, are almost all black and middle class. In Queens, the median black household income is higher than the median white household income—$34,300 a year compared to $34,000 a year. Howard Beach is just west of Kennedy Airport. It became famous some years ago when a white mob killed a black man there. Ozone Park, just north of it, has houses in rows so snug you can hardly see the seams between them,

and each house has a lawn the size of a living-room rug:
some of the lawns are bordered by brick fences with stat-
uettes of elephants raising their trunks, some are thick with
flowers, some with ornamental shrubs in rows. People water
in the mornings there and get down on all fours to pick
pieces of detritus from the grass. In front of 107-44 110th
Street, a house with gray siding and black trim and a picture
window, several men came up to the owner, Joseph Scopo,
as he got out of a car one night in 1993, and they shot him
a number of times. He made it across the street and died
near the stone-front house at 107-35. The front yard of
Mr. Scopo's former house is all cement; for many years, he
was the vice president of Local 6A of the Cement and Concrete Workers of New York City.

On Kissena Boulevard, in Flushing, I passed a two-story
brick row house with a dentist's office on the first floor and
the sign "D. D. Dong, D.M.D." By now, my feet were hurt-
ing and my legs were chafed and I was walking oddly. At the
end of a sunlit alley, a pink turban leaned under the hood
of a yellow cab. A yellow-and-black butterfly flew over a
muffler-repair shop. A red rose grew through coils of razor
wire and chain-link fence. At a juicing machine on the street,
I bought an almost-cool Styrofoam cup of sugarcane juice,
grassy tasting and sweet. Then I was among the Cold War ru-
ins of Flushing Meadow Park, site of the 1964–65 World's
Fair, which is now a mostly empty expanse coexisting with
about half a dozen freeways at the borough's heart. No place
I know of in America looks more like Moscow than Flushing Meadow Park: the heroic, forgotten statuary, all flexed
muscle and straining toes; the littered grounds buffed by feet

to smooth dirt; the vast broken fountains, with their twisted pipes and puddles of olive-colored water. I leaned on the railing of a large, unexplained concrete pool thick with floating trash and watched a sparrow on a soda can do a quick logrolling number to stay on top. No matter what, I could not get out of my mind "D. D. Dong, D.M.D."

Legally, you can buy wigs made of human hair in Queens, and two-hundred-volt appliances designed to work in the outlets in foreign countries, and T-shirts that say "If you can't get enough, get a Guyanese," and extra-extra-large bulletproof vests with side panels, and pink bikini underwear with the New York Police Department shield and "New York's Hottest" printed on the front, and pepper-spray personal-defense canisters with ultraviolet identifying dye added, and twenty-ounce bottles of Laser Malt Liquor, whose slogan is "Beam me up," and a cut-rate ten-minute phone call to just about any place on earth, and a viewing of the Indian movie *Sabse Bade Khiladi*, featuring "the hottest song of 1995, 'Muqubla Muqubla.' " Illegally, if you know how, you can buy drugs in bulk, especially cocaine. Drug enforcement officers say that Queens is one of the main entry points for cocaine in the United States and that much of the trade is engineered by Colombians in the neighborhoods of Elmhurst and Jackson Heights, a district called Little Colombia. On the Elmhurst–Jackson Heights border, at Eighty-third Street just below the Roosevelt Avenue El, is a pocket-sized park of trees and benches called Manuel de

Dios Unanue Triangle. It is named for a journalist killed in Queens in 1992 by agents of a Colombian drug cartel.

Manuel de Dios Unanue was born in Cuba, graduated from the University of Puerto Rico, and worked as a newspaper reporter in New York. In 1984, he became the editor of *El Diario–La Prensa*, the city's largest Spanish-language newspaper. At *El Diario*, he was, according to various accounts, obsessive, crusading, blindly self-righteous, possessed of a brilliant news sense, delusional, uncompromising, vain. He chain-smoked. He believed that the United States should open political discussions with Castro, a view that angered anticommunist terrorist groups, and he printed many articles about the drug trade. He received death threats with a regularity that became a joke between him and his colleagues. Once, someone painted black zebra stripes on his white car and left a note saying he would "get it."

In the eighties and the early nineties, drug money flowed into Queens. Police said that check-cashing places and travel agencies and other businesses in Elmhurst and Jackson Heights were laundering it. Steamer trunks full of submachine guns traced to a realty company on Queens Boulevard led to the discovery of apartments with stashes of drugs and money elsewhere in the city. Colombians died by violence in Queens all the time. One year, 44 of the borough's 357 homicide victims were Colombians. Pedro Méndez, a political figure who had raised money for the 1990 campaign of Colombia's new antidrug president, was shot to death near his home in Jackson Heights the night before that president's inauguration. At a pay telephone by a florist's shop on Northern Boulevard, police arrested a man named Dandeny Muñoz-Mosquera, who they said was an assassin wanted for crimes that included the murders of at least forty police officers in Colombia. Although the authorities believed he had come to Queens to kill somebody, at his arrest they could hold him only for giving a false name to a federal officer. In prison, he requested that Manuel de Dios do an interview with him.

Manuel de Dios had left *El Diario* by then, fired in 1989 for reckless reporting, according to some accounts. On his own, he wrote (and published) a book called *The Secrets of the Medellin Cartel*, an antidrug exposé. He began to publish two magazines, *Cambio XXI* and *Crimen*, in which he identified alleged drug traffickers and dealers and the local places where they did business, with big photographs. In Colombia, some people—according to federal agents, José Santacruz Londono and Gilberto Rodríguez-Orejula, of the Cali drug cartel, among others—decided to have him killed. Someone hired someone and his wife, who hired someone, who hired Wilson Alejandro Mejía Vélez, a sixteen-year-old employee of a chair factory in Staten Island. One afternoon the boy put on a hood, walked into the Mesón Asturias restaurant in Queens, and shot Manuel de Dios twice in the back of the head as he finished a beer at the bar.

The Times, The New Yorker, Salman Rushdie, and others decried the murder. Police said they would solve it soon, and sixteen months after the killing, on a tip from an informant, they caught the killer and some of the conspirators, not including the higher-ups in Colombia. The killer and four others stood trial, were convicted, and went to jail. The triggerboy got life without parole. Manuel de Dios's magazines ceased publication after his death. His book cannot be found in the Spanish-language bookstores in Elmhurst, or *Books in Print*. People in Elmhurst know the name of the book, and they say the name of its author in a familiar rush, but they cannot tell you where you might find a copy. Recently, the number of local drug-related murders has gone down; people say this is because the victory of one big drug cartel over another has brought stability to the trade.

The Mesón Asturias restaurant is just across Eighty-third Street from the Manuel de Dios Unanue Triangle. On a hot July afternoon, I went into the restaurant, sat down at the bar, and had a beer. The bartender, a short, trim man with dark hair, put a bowl of peanuts by me and cut some slices of chorizo sausage. We watched Spanish TV on cable and commented on a piece about the running of the bulls at Pamplona. The bartender said that an American had been killed and that you had to know how to be with the bulls. I paid for the beer and got up to leave. I asked, "Is this where the journalist was killed?"

"Oh, yes," the bartender said.

"Were you here?"

"No, I was outside."

"Did you know him?"

"Yes, he was a regular."

"He must have been a brave man," I said.

The bartender stood not facing me and not facing away. He pushed the dollar I had left for a tip across the bar, and I pushed it back at him. For a while the bartender looked off toward the dim, gated window. "Well," he said, "you never know your luck."

The oldest house in Queens—perhaps in the city—is a frame farmhouse built in 1661 by a man who later suffered banishment for letting Quakers meet there. His neighbors in the town of Flushing sent the Dutch governor a remonstrance stating their belief in religious freedom not only for Quakers and other Christians but also for "Jews, Turks, and Egyptians." Today, the house, called the Bowne House, sits on a small patch of lawn between a four-story apartment building and a city playground. The theoretical Jews, Turks, and Egyptians are now real and living nearby, but nearest are the Koreans. Almost all the signs you see in downtown Flushing are in Korean, and the neighborhood has a Quaker meetinghouse, Korean Buddhist temples, and Korean Catholic and Protestant churches. At the end of the No. 7 Flushing subway line, pamphleteers for a city council person hand you flyers saying that the line is going to hell, while other people hand you fundamentalist Christian tracts saying that you are. Pentecostal churches in storefronts all over Queens have signs in the window advising, for example, "Do nothing you would not like to be doing when Jesus comes," in Spanish and English. A multimillion-dollar Hindu temple, the largest in the city, recently went up in Flushing. Many Hindus, Buddhists, and Sikhs have recently added small celebrations of Christmas to their traditional worship calendars. Groups of Gnostics meet in Queens, and Romanian Baptists, and followers of the guru Sri Chinmoy, who sometimes express their faith by doing enough somersaults to get into the *Guinness Book of World Records*. When summer comes, big striped tents rise on outlying vacant lots with billboards advertising tent meeting revivals led by Pastor John H. Boyd.

In Douglaston, a far Queens neighborhood that still has the feel of a town, I sat on the lawn of an Episcopal church at the crest of a hill. The ancient gravestones in the churchyard leaned, the daylilies along the driveway bloomed, and the white wooden church panted discreetly in the heat through its high open windows. In Astoria, I visited St. Irene's of Chrysovalantou Greek Orthodox Church, home of the icon of St. Irene, which witnesses say wept on the eve of the Persian Gulf War. A short woman all in black said, "Why not? Why not?" when I asked if I could see the icon, and she led me slowly up the aisle in fragrant, dusky church light. The icon, a six-by-eight-inch painting, is in a large frame made of gold bracelets, jeweled wristwatches, and rows of wedding rings donated by parishioners. On a wooden rail below it are inhalers left by asthma sufferers whose breath St. Irene has restored. In Richmond Hill, I stopped in at Familiar Pharmacy, managed and co-owned by Mohammad Tayyab, who knows the Qur'an by heart. He is thirty-nine, has a neatly trimmed beard, and wears his baseball cap backward. He told me that, growing up in Multan, Pakistan, he memorized verses from the Qur'an almost every day, morning to night, from when he was six until he was twelve. The Qur'an is about the length of the New Testament. A person who knows the Qur'an by heart is called a *haviz*. Mohammad Tayyab recites the whole Qur'an once a year in a mosque during the fast of Ramadan and reviews three chapters every night, to keep fresh. The stored-up energy of his knowledge causes him to radiate, like a person who has just been to a spa.

In Montefiore Cemetery, in another far part of Queens, the Grand Rebbe of the Lubavitcher Hasidim, Menachem Schneerson, lies in a coffin made of boards from his lectern. By the time of Rebbe Schneerson's death, in 1994, at the age of ninety-three, some of his followers had come to believe he was the Messiah. Tens of thousands of Lubavitchers from around the world have visited his grave, sometimes annoying the black families who own homes nearby. Neighbors complained that the Lubavitchers were singing loudly, drinking beer, trespassing, and asking to use their bathrooms. The sect has since bought a house near the grave for the convenience of visitors. I went to see the grave myself, on an anniversary of the rebbe's death. Cars with out-of-state plates lined the boulevard by the cemetery gate; some cars had their doors open to the curb, and shoeless Lubavitchers lay asleep on the seats. Along the paths to the grave site ran that orange-webbed plastic security fence in which we now routinely wrap important public events. Some of the Lubavitchers were pink-cheeked teens with blond side curls. Cops not much older leaned against the cemetery gate and smoked, thumbs hooked in their belts, cigarettes between their first two fingers.

Black-clad Lubavitchers in black hats were coming and going. In the patio behind the nearby Lubavitcher house, many were reciting prayers. Occasionally, an impassioned voice would rise like a firework bursting higher than the others. A man about my age who pointed the way to the grave suggested that I remove my shoes before approaching it; "Remember, this is a holy place," he said. My running shoes looked as bright as a television ad on top of the pile of functional black brogans of many sizes already there. I ducked through a low door to an anteroom filled with candles. It led into an enclosure of walls maybe twelve feet high and open to the sky. At the center of the enclosure was a knee-high wall around the grave itself. Men were standing at the graveside wall and praying, chanting, flipping expertly through small prayer books in their palms, rocking from side to side with the words. Heaped on top of the grave like raked-up leaves, spilling onto the smooth pebbles next to it, drifting into the anteroom, were hundreds or thousands of small square pieces of paper on which people had written prayers for special intercessions. There are so many hopes in the world. Just out of the line of sight past the higher wall, 747s descended slowly to Kennedy Airport like local elevators stopping at every floor. Across the street just out of earshot, long-legged girls jumped double-Dutch jump rope, superfast.

(1996)

TYPEWRITER MAN

I write on a manual typewriter, but don't bug me about it, okay? I know that recently certain machines have been developed that produce manuscripts more efficiently than a manual typewriter ever could. When these machines began to take over, people constantly asked if I used one; for a while that was the fact about me people seemed most interested to know. When I replied that I didn't, people usually became vexed, or in some cases nearly enraged. The arguments that followed were of a pattern. Those in favor of the new machines described their many advantages, never failing to include the ease with which the new machines could move paragraphs around. I defended myself with explanations that started out mild and reasonable and quickly descended to a whiny "I just don't like them!" None of this got anybody anywhere. Then one day a champion of the new machines pinned me down on the subject, extolling them, as usual, and finally confronting me with the inevitable question: Did I use one? My panic began to mount as I saw what lay ahead—the arguments, the rebuttals, the recriminations. I took a deep breath. "No . . . I mean, *yes!*" I replied. Satisfied, the prosecutor moved on to other topics, as my heart rate returned to normal.

Then suddenly that question was not around anymore. No one has asked me it in years. I guess the victory of the new machines has been so complete that there's no longer a need to hunt down resisters. Why bother? Time will take care of us. Meanwhile, I continued to write on the same Olympia portable manual I had bought with my first paycheck from *Oui* magazine, in Chicago in 1973. I liked it so much that when I got a little money I bought other Olympia manuals, fancier models, but all of them used, of course. They are perhaps not the best manual typewriters ever made—experts often give that distinction to Underwoods or Hermes—but they suit me, and I've stuck by them. The hell of it is, though, that after about twenty years they start to break. One afternoon in 1994 the "e" key on my favorite Olympia stopped working. "E" is not a rarity, like @ or %, that you can mostly do without. I was living in Brooklyn at the time. I called around and found a guy there who claimed to be able to fix anything, typewriters included. When he returned the typewriter to me, all the keys were at different heights, like notes in a lilting tune, and the "e" bar hit the ribbon hard enough to make a mark only if you helped it with your finger.

The Manhattan Yellow Pages has so many listings under "Typewriters" that you might think getting someone to fix a manual would not be hard. The repair places I called were agreeable enough at first, but as I described the problem (*Fixing an "e," for Pete's sake! How tough can that be?*), they began to hedge and temporize. They mentioned a scarcity of spare parts, and the difficulty of welding forged steel, and other problems, all apparently my own fault for not having foreseen. I took my typewriter various places to have it looked at and brought it home again unrepaired. This went on for a while. Finally, approaching the end of the Yellow Pages listing, I found an entry for "TYTELL TYPWRTR CO." It advertised restorations of antiques, an on-premises machine shop, a huge inventory of manuals, and sixty-five years of experience and accumulated parts. The address was in lower Manhattan. I called the number, and a voice answered, "Martin Tytell." I told Mr. Tytell my problem, and he told me he certainly could fix it. I said I would bring the typewriter in next week. "You should bring it in as soon as possible," he advised. "I'm an old man."

I got on the subway to Fulton Street right away and carried my typewriter up the stairs to his second-floor shop at 116 Fulton. I saw that he was indeed an old man, standing on a teetering stepladder and moving a heavy typewriter onto a high shelf while a woman's voice offstage told him to be careful and reminded him of his recent heart surgery. He climbed down and shook my hand. He was wearing a clean white lab coat over a light-blue shirt and a dark-blue bow tie. His head was almost bald on top and fringed with white professor-style side hairs that matched the white of his small mustache. His blue eyes were slitted and wary and humorous, and all his features had a sharpness produced by a lifetime of focusing concentration down to pica size. He examined the typewriter and gave me a claim check and told me I could pick it up in a few days. His shop fixed the "e" and completely overhauled the machine and got it running better than it ever had.

I ended up going back to see Mr. Tytell many times. I moved from New York to a distant part of the country, but when I returned for visits I brought typewriters for him to repair. I met his wife, Pearl, and their son, Peter, who's fifty-two. Both Pearl and Peter are handwriting and document experts who often testify in court cases where written evidence is involved. Mr. and Mrs. Tytell have been married for fifty-four years. Pearl Tytell is handsome and petite, with unwavering blue eyes and long silver-blond hair, which she wears in a braid wrapped carefully on the top of her head. For clothes she favors suits in subdued colors or pleated skirts in dark plaid, and neat white blouses with a cameo brooch at the throat. She looks like someone you would believe on the witness stand. Her habit of accuracy provides running footnotes to the autobiography her husband likes to tell. The shop is mostly floor-to-ceiling shelves of typewriters in cases or wrapped in plastic sheets, boxes of typewriter parts past numbering, and disassembled typewriters on benches, all in a labyrinthine layout beneath fluorescent lights. Mr. Tytell works in one part of the shop and his wife in another, invisible but nearby among the shelves.

When my father was a communications officer on aircraft carriers in the Second World War, he sent his family letters typewritten on flyweight airmail stationery. He single-spaced and made almost no mistakes. To his younger brother in the hospital he described everything about the ship

Boxer—the war had ended by then, and censorship had eased—that caught his eye, from the shadow of the bridge moving through the clear depths to the formations of the fighter planes above. His ship was the flagship of a convoy and so carried both a captain and an admiral. He described how the one would send the other a message via the communications room, to be typed up in many copies and passed along in a procedure that took a long time, especially considering that the two men were at command posts separated by just a flight of stairs. He brought home sheaves of navy documents in his sea chest. Many were stamped TOP SE-CRET in red ink and had holes punched in them and signatures affixed. They had to do with maneuvers and requests obscure to me, and the capture of a German submarine. They were on paper so light you could almost see through it, and their carbon-copy typescript was fuzzy and thick.

My father used a stand-up Royal typewriter, green with a tortoiseshell finish, and its type was small and clear. I remember him sitting with his hands poised over it, little fingers out to the sides, typing what I now know was a description of one of his patents or a letter of complaint to the Ford Motor Company. If one of my sisters or brothers or I lost a baby tooth, we always put it in an envelope under our pillow. When we woke in the morning, the tooth would have been replaced by a dollar bill and a letter from the tooth fairy. Generally these letters discussed some bureaucratic problem the tooth fairy was having with his lost-tooth filing system or with a secretary who had recently gotten pregnant and quit. The letters were neatly typed in the same clear print as on my father's Royal. He did not like me to fool with the typewriter, but I tried to use it when I barely knew how to write by hand. It always surprised me what a bad job I did and what a mess I made. Somehow I always had to get my fingers into the works, tangling the typewriter ribbon and smearing ink and detaching the spool. Like the sound of a typewriter bell, that smell of an inked silk type-writer ribbon, a smell combining sootiness with a medicinal volatility, has almost vanished today.

In Mr. Tytell's shop, of course, it is in good supply. I can't say that when I breathe it there, impressions of the past come to me in a conscious or orderly way. It's deeper than that—as if I had opened my father's sea chest again and stuck my head into its stored-up aura of 1940s wartime. Mr. Tytell understands that his trade involves more than just some possibly out-of-date office machines. "We don't get normal people here," he says with a certain pride. Coincidentally or not, the second time I saw him he made a point of showing me a small typewriter in a steel case as smooth and silvery as a gun mount on an airplane wing. He told me it was an un-crushable typewriter case designed during the Second World War to survive being run over by a tank. Then he began to tell me his experiences working on typewriters for the gov-ernment during the war.

The Second World War was a manual-typewriter war. One would be tempted to say that never will typewriters be nearly so important in a war again, were it not for the many manual typewriters in the Serbian and Croatian alphabets that Mr. Tytell has sold for use in Bosnia in recent years. Armies in the Second World War took typewriters with them into battle and typed with them in the field on little tripod stands. In the United States, typewriters were classified as wartime matériel, under the control of the War Production Board and unavailable for purchase by civilians without special authorization. Among the ships sunk off Normandy during the D-day invasion was a cargo ship carrying twenty thousand Royal and Underwood typewriters intended for the use of the Allies. Mr. Tytell says that as far as he knows, all twenty thousand are still down there. More than other veterans, a man whose life has been typewriters is likely to divide his history into short summaries covering before the war and after the war, and volumes in between.

Martin Tytell was born to Russian Jewish parents in New York in 1913, and he grew up on Rutgers Street, on the Lower East Side. He was the ninth of ten children, seven of whom survived. His father had come to America from Argentina, where he manufactured wheels for the Argentine government. In New York he worked as a machinist. Martin always loved tools and screws, and he began working in a hardware store when he was still a boy. He carried a screwdriver wherever he went. One day in gym class at Thomas Jefferson High School, the assignment was rope climbing, which Martin thought was for monkeys, so he got the teacher to let him spend the period in a nearby office answering the phone. The office had an Underwood No. 5 typewriter, which Martin began to examine and take apart. That kind of Underwood was designed so that just a single screw disconnected the carriage, to allow for basic cleaning and maintenance without disturbing the rest of the machine. The screw was hard to put back in, however, so Martin had to leave the typewriter in pieces. This happened several times. Finally the repairman who came to fix the Underwood went looking for the kid who was taking it apart. He ended up offering to teach Martin how to work on Underwoods at his apartment in Canarsie. Martin went there for six Sundays in a row. Soon he could take an Underwood apart and put it together blindfolded, a trick that won him the account for maintenance of all the typewriters at Columbia-Presbyterian Hospital when he went there one day cold-canvassing for a job. Before he was out of high school, he had several other accounts to maintain typewriters around the city, and his own office at 206 Broadway.

The records of his present business go back to 1935. By then he had moved to an office at 87 Nassau Street, which he left a few years later for 123 Fulton Street, which he left in 1964 for where he is now. As well as fixing typewriters, he had them for rent and sold them new and used. Pearl came to work for him in 1938. At about that time he added a new service to his business—converting American-made typewriters to foreign alphabets for the stationery department at Macy's department store. He did these jobs on short notice and fast. Macy's would tell a customer that they could provide a typewriter in the customer's language before he left town; then Martin would remove the type from an American typewriter, solder on new type for the alphabet desired, and put new lettering on the keyboard. Usually he converted to Spanish or French, not difficult jobs, but he did Russian, Greek, and German, too. He found that by adding an idle gear he bought for forty-five cents on Canal Street, he could make a typewriter go from right to left. That enabled him to do Arabic and other right-left languages such as Hebrew and Farsi.

Nights he took courses in business administration at St. John's University. When a recruiter came and made a pitch about the Marine Corps to the students there, Martin decided to join the Marine Corps Reserves, hoping to go on to flight school and become a navy pilot. He did his basic training at Quantico and then served part-time at bases in the New York area. On his own he took flying lessons at an airfield on Staten Island. Pearl took lessons too; they courted while learning to fly. Pearl briefly considered becoming a ferry pilot for the military. Martin earned high marks on the entrance tests for flight school but in the end didn't get in. The official reason was his flat feet. He thinks he would have made a good pilot, and that the real reason was cultural— that the navy preferred Waspy Ivy League types. The officer who signed his honorable-discharge papers in November of 1940 told him privately that "night-college guys" like him generally did not do well in flight school.

Factories that make typewriters use the same equipment and methods as factories that make guns. By the time the United States had entered the war, most American typewriter manufacturers had changed over to the production of things like bombsights and rifle barrels. Much as the war needed typewriters, it needed guns more. The lack of new typewriters sent the War Department scrambling for whatever machines it could find, in whatever shape; this led naturally to the shop of Martin Tytell. His sales business was nonexistent and his income from rentals slim, and he began to do more and more work for the government, fixing up used machines. In 1943 the War Department got a windfall of Remington typewriters designed originally to be sold in Siam. By then Martin was back in the service, in the army this time, so Pearl (by then Mrs. Tytell) went down to the Pentagon and examined the machines and saw that they could be converted from Siamese to what the military required. An official of the War Production Board who had been an executive for a big typewriter wholesaler in the Midwest got Martin transferred from Fort Jay, on Governors Island, to a detached-duty unit called the Enlisted Reserve Corps for ninety days' service. Martin did the work on the Remingtons in his shop on Fulton Street while spending his nights at home.

From the kinds of typewriter jobs he was asked to do, and especially from the alphabets involved, Martin could make good guesses about upcoming strategy in the war. He predicted to the day the landing at Normandy. For a private first class, he saw the war effort on an unusually big screen, as he kept the typewriters working at Fort Jay and at the Manhattan offices of *Yank* magazine and at recruiting stations in the city and upstate. He spent much of his time assigned to the army's Morale Services Division, at 165 Broadway, which dealt in information and propaganda. There he received his hardest job of the war—a rush request to convert typewriters to twenty-one different languages of Asia and the South Pacific. Many of the languages he had never heard of before. The War Department wanted to provide airmen, in case they were shot down, with survival kits that included messages on silk in the languages of people they were likely to meet on the ground. Morale Services found native speakers and scholars to help with the languages. Martin obtained the type and did the soldering and the keyboards. The implications of the work and its difficulty brought him to near collapse, but he completed it with only one mistake: on the Burmese typewriter he put a letter on upside down. Years later, after he had discovered his error, he told the language professor he had worked with that he would fix that letter on the professor's Burmese typewriter. The professor said not to bother; in the intervening years, as a result of typewriters copied from Martin's original, that upside-down letter had been accepted in Burma as proper typewriter style.

When Martin received his honorable discharge, in November of 1945, the colonel of his unit gave him a testimonial dinner and a typewriter ribbon done up in the style of a military decoration. Being a civilian made little change in what Martin did every day. He still worked on typewriters for the government, and since manufacture had not yet resumed, he scared up serviceable used ones just as before. For a while he was running an assembly line by car, carrying parts in his trunk to mechanics all over New York who had worked in typewriter factories and knew certain steps of the process. He hired more assistants at his shop, including some displaced persons recently arrived from Europe. One of them had escaped from a concentration camp and hidden in the house of a farmer; he worked for Martin for years and sent the farmer a package of food and clothes every month for as long as Martin knew him. Another had learned typewriter repair in Germany before the war, a skill that kept him alive at Auschwitz, where he was given the job of converting to German a large number of Russian typewriters looted by the Germans along the eastern front. After the Soviet Army liberated the camp, the Russians had him convert the typewriters back to Russian again.

The history of the typewriter from its invention to the present is complicated, but not that complicated. Where you can get lost is in discussions about who made the first writing machine—there are a lot of candidates, in Europe and in the early United States—and in lists of the many typewriters patented and manufactured in the years after the machines caught on. It's easier to say who made the first typewriter that led eventually to commercial success: in 1873 E. Remington & Sons, gunmakers of Ilion, New York, began production of an up-strike typewriter with a four-bank keyboard based on a machine developed a few years before by the Wisconsin inventors Carlos Glidden and Christopher Latham Sholes. The company made 550 typewriters the first year; Mark Twain bought one. People said the typewriter would never replace the pen, but in offices it soon did. Its popularity gave women a way to enter the workforce in large numbers for the first time. For a while their name, "type writers," was the same as the machines'. The typewriter gets some credit for contributing to the movement for women's suffrage and emancipation at the turn of the century. By that time more than thirty companies were making typewriters in the United States, and the typewriter bell had become a commonplace business sound. Remington

& Sons sold its typewriter division in 1886, but its name appeared on manual typewriters for almost a hundred years.

The Remington and other early machines were sometimes called "blind writers," because the paper disappeared down into the works and the type struck the paper where it couldn't be seen. A German-born inventor named Franz Xavier Wagner thought that an upright machine whose type hit the paper in sight would be a better idea. He invented one and took his "visible writer" to Remington, but the company wasn't interested. Wagner founded a company and began making the machines himself in the mid-1890s. Their obvious superiority to the blind writers won the market in a few years, and every typewriter company began to make variations on Wagner's design. With that the basic technology of the manual typewriter was in place and would remain unchanged. The company Wagner founded soon became the Underwood Typewriter Company, of New York and Connecticut. America produced many other fine makes of typewriter—Royal, Hammond, Corona—but the Underwood would remain the industry standard for the rest of the manual typewriter's reign.

By the 1920s about half of all typewriters sold in the world were Underwoods. Typewriter technology moved on to refinements, with machines that were quieter or lighter or easier on the fingertips. Oddly, no typewriter manufacturer succeeded in improving on one of the most inefficient features of the original machines—the arrangement of the keyboard. Almost all typewriters used the Universal keyboard, also called the QWERTY keyboard, which dated from the experimental machines of Glidden and Sholes. Remington had copied its keyboard from their model, and other manufacturers copied Remington. Today no one can say for sure why Glidden and Sholes arranged the keys that way. Their three-tier layout of letters, with an apparently random selection on the top line, a quasi-alphabetical-order segment as part of the middle line, and more randomness on the bottom, resists persuasive explanation. As the machinery improved and typing speeds increased, the awkwardness of the keyboard became plain. An industry conference met in 1905 and considered ideas for better keyboards, without result. In 1932 a professor at the University of Washington named August Dvorak introduced a statistics-based keyboard arrangement that he said improved typing speed over the Universal by 35 percent. He spent decades trying to get his keyboard accepted but finally concluded that it would be as easy to change the Golden Rule. There just never was a moment when enough people who knew how to type were willing to learn all over again. The QWERTY layout survived on manual typewriters and slid effortlessly onto electric typewriters and beyond. Today, no matter what kind of machine you write on, the QWERTY, a "primitive tortureboard" according to Dvorak, is probably the keyboard you use.

As a maker of manual typewriters, America declined after the Second World War. Production never returned to what it had been; from being the world's largest exporter of typewriters, the United States became the largest importer. The postwar years brought the rise of typewriter companies in countries where peaceful manufacturing was encouraged while we continued to make guns—Nippon in Japan,

Olympia in West Germany, and Olivetti in Italy. Olympia and Olivetti quickly grew to multinational giants. Olympia built typewriter factories in Yugoslavia, Canada, Mexico, and Chile. Olivetti, which had been making typewriters since 1911, expanded into England and the United States. In 1959 it bought Underwood and eventually phased out that famous name. By the mid–1960s manual typewriters had begun to disappear owing to the success of the electric typewriter, an invention that would have its own saga of rise and decline. No one has made manual typewriters in America for decades. The European companies have mostly discontinued their manual lines and moved into various electronic machines. For someone interested in buying a brand-new manual typewriter, a hundred-plus years of typewriter history comes down to this: Olympia still makes a small portable, Olivetti makes two portables and a heavier office machine, and the largest manufacturer of English-language manual typewriters in the world seems to be the Godrej & Boyce Manufacturing Company of India, located on the outskirts of Bombay.

Mr. Tytell goes to his shop two or three days a week, depending on how he's feeling. Customers who want to see him call his answering machine, and he calls back and sets up appointments. A sign on the wall that says

PSYCHOANALYSIS FOR YOUR TYPEWRITER
WHETHER IT'S FRUSTRATED, INHIBITED, SCHIZOID
OR WHAT HAVE YOU

contributes to the doctor-patient quality of the visits. Plus he's wearing a white lab coat and you're not. Some customers arrive in limousines, which wait nearby until the sessions are through. Mr. Tytell has fixed typewriters for such people as Perle Mesta and the archbishop of Lebanon and Charles Kuralt. Some customers climb sweating from the subway station and stop for a moment in the daylight of Fulton Street to switch the case containing the heavy machine from one hand to the other. Because of a mishap involving a romance novelist, a treasured typewriter, and the wreck of a parcel-service truck, Mr. Tytell now refuses to ship typewriters under any circumstances. Getting a typewriter repaired by him is a hands-on, person-to-person deal.

Several afternoons last spring I sat on a swiveling typing chair by the clear space on the table where Mr. Tytell lets people test their typewriters before taking them home, and he and Mrs. Tytell and I talked. "People get very emotionally involved with their typewriters," Mr. Tytell said. "I understand it—I talk to typewriters myself sometimes. On the one hand, you have people who love a machine for whatever reason. On the other, sometimes you find a person with an extreme dislike, almost a hatred, for a particular machine. It's funny how the two go together. Recently I got a call from a lady and she had a portable typewriter, like new, and she wanted it out of her apartment right away. It's from a divorce or something; I didn't ask. She's not selling it, she says she'll pay *me* if I'll just come and take it away. Well, three hours earlier I had gotten a call from another lady; her husband had just lost a typewriter he loved, somebody stole it, and it was the exact same make and model this other lady described. So I went and picked up the machine, and when I got back, I called the other lady, and she rushed right down and bought it and carried it out the door. She was overjoyed.

"People hug and kiss me when I fix their typewriters sometimes. That call just now was from a lady I did a Latvian typewriter for—she was so happy I could hardly get her off the phone. I don't know why, a typewriter touches something inside. A couple—she's the secretary to the Episcopal church in Manhattan—brought in an old Underwood for an overhaul, and I made it sing, and they came by the shop with coffee and cake to thank me, and the husband wrote me a poem in iambic pentameter. It's called 'Tytell, the Wizard King of Fulton Street.' You see, people get carried away. They write me letters, they send me fruit baskets, they give me miniature typewriters made out of porcelain. Almost everybody I deal with is an interesting person of some kind. Here's an invoice for a job I did for the only harp mechanic in the New York area, a guy who tunes and repairs harps, and he's decided he wants to translate Homer from the original Greek, and he wants me to make a typewriter in Homeric Greek for him. That's no problem—I've done ancient-Greek typewriters before. I even did a typewriter in hieroglyphics one time, for a curator at the Brooklyn Museum."

On a shelf across the table, just at eye level, was a typewriter bearing the Exxon logo. It looked big and black enough to spill ink all over Alaska, and I asked about it. Mr. Tytell said that the oil company manufactured its own brand of electric typewriters briefly some years ago; he keeps this one for its oddity, and for parts. Then, back among the windings of his shop, he showed me the century in type-writers: a 1910 Hammond portable, with a keyboard that folded out on hinges and hung suspended in air; a Smith Premier Monarch of the 1920s, as solid and imposing as a safe; a Remington Noiseless from 1938, on which the type bar just kisses the roller, or platen, and the keys respond to the lightest touch; a Woodstock typewriter from the 1940s or 1950s, the brand sold for many years by Sears & Roe-buck, on which Godrej & Boyce modeled the first manual typewriters it made; a TelePrompTer typewriter of the kind formerly used by TV studios to type up scripts for scrolling on TV monitors. Newer technology has made TelePrompTers obsolete, but Mr. Tytell still sells a few of them, usually to organizations that help the hard of seeing, who like the out-size type.

We sidled through right angles into a dark and cramped part of the shop where we had to proceed by flashlight. "In these cabinets reposes the largest collection of foreign type in the world—a hundred and forty-five languages, over two million separate pieces of type," he said, sweeping the beam over banks of minutely labeled metal drawers. Sixty years of converting typewriters to different alphabets has amassed this inventory; Mr. Tytell can list man's written languages better perhaps than any nontenured person in the world. "Over there are some languages of India—Hindi, Sindhi, Marathi, Punjabi, and Sanskrit—and next to that is Coptic, a church language of the Middle East; it's a beautiful-looking thing. Then there's Hausa, a language nobody here has ever heard of, spoken by twenty million people in northern Nigeria.

Over there's Korean, and the Siamese I took off those Remingtons during the war, which I've relabeled Thai, and Aramaic script, and Hebrew, and Yiddish . . ." He pointed out with the flashlight drawers of Malay and Armenian and Amharic, and boxes of special symbols for pharmacists and mathematicians. One drawer seemed to be mostly umlauts. He opened it and took out a small orange cardboard box and shone the light on the dozens of mint-bright rectangles of steel inside, each with its two tiny raised dots. "Nobody else in the world would even bother with this stuff," he said.

We wandered to a better-lit area of shelves filled with IBM Selectric typewriters circa 1970. The Selectric was to electric typewriters what the Underwood was to manuals, and it also is extinct. It has an equally dedicated following; fixing Selectrics is a lively part of Mr. Tytell's business. Mrs. Tytell, who had been on the phone, joined us. I asked Mr. and Mrs. Tytell what machine, of all the manual and electric typewriters ever made, they thought was the best. Mrs. Tytell said you couldn't really compare manuals and electrics. "I'm prejudiced," Mr. Tytell said, "because I spent so many years servicing Underwoods. Actually, I love all typewriters the same, but an Underwood manual with a serial number in the eight millions"—he climbed riskily onto a stepladder at another shelf and shakily handed one down—"which would be an Underwood made around 1959, is a beautiful machine." He pulled away the plastic that wrapped the typewriter. Its grayish-beige buffed finish, still in good shape, was pure 1959.

Mrs. Tytell tapped her clear-lacquered fingernail on a key in the upper right-hand corner of the keyboard. The key had a plus sign on top and an equal sign below. "This key on this particular kind of typewriter was the deciding piece of evidence in a multimillion-dollar fraud case I worked on a few years ago," she said. "A younger son of a wealthy man had been specifically excluded from inheriting some theaters the father had owned. An assignment document, typewritten and with the father's signature, gave the theaters to the older sons instead. The younger son was twelve when his father died, and he always felt that his father wouldn't have done that to him, because his father used to take him to these theaters all the time. The younger son grew up and became a lawyer and pursued this question, and finally he came to me with the assignment document, and I found that it was typed on an Underwood of this particular model and year. The assignment document had no plus or equal signs on it, but I was able to prove that the machine that had typed it also typed other documents that did have those signs, and that was the clincher. Underwood didn't add that particular key to their keyboard until well after the document in question was supposed to have been signed. When I explained all this to the lawyer for the older brothers, he said, 'So what?' A few weeks later they settled out of court for a lot of money."

In the 1980s Mrs. Tytell provided important evidence in the income-tax-evasion trial of the religious leader Sun Myung Moon. To prove that more than a million dollars in bank deposits were church assets and not personal funds, Moon had produced a number of dated documents. Mrs. Tytell, who studied at the Institute of Paper Chemistry, examined the paper the documents were printed on, and eventually learned what mill had made the paper and what year it was made. Certain intricacies of the papermaking process meant she could have learned the month it was made and maybe even the day, but that wasn't necessary. The paper dated from a year after the date on the documents. "It was what you call a slam dunk," Mrs. Tytell said. Moon went to jail for about a year.

When I remarked to Mr. and Mrs. Tytell that I had seen a certain manual typewriter for sale in a pawnshop in South Dakota, they said, simultaneously, "Buy it!" They said that you never see manual typewriters in pawnshops or at flea markets anymore. Suddenly typewriters have become valuable, and they turn up in museums and antique shows and Hollywood prop-company warehouses. Collectors see typewriters disappearing over the horizon and grab for them. Collecting may become a bigger part of the Tytells' business; Peter Tytell regards old typewriters as holy, and tells his parents to hang on to them, and is an avid collector himself. The thought of the typewriter's approaching antiquity reminds me of what happened to Latin, another antiquity. Once Latin was safely dead as a language, it acquired an appeal for scientists and others not only for its precision but because it would remain forever unchanged. Maybe the perfection in form and function of a 1959 Underwood manual will have a similar appeal for people who want a writing system they won't ever have to upgrade. Before I left Mr. Tytell, I asked him if he thought that the manual typewriter would survive.

"I'm eighty-three years old and I just signed a ten-year lease on this office," he said. "I'm an optimist, obviously. I hope they do survive—manual typewriters are where my heart is: they're what keep me alive. What's so intriguing about a manual typewriter is that it's all right there in front of you—all the thought that went into it, all these really smart guys that worked on it and gave their lives for it. The way these machines continue to function, it really is a miracle. You see some old beat-up machine in an attic or someplace and you touch the keys and it still works fine. Companies still make typewriter ribbons—the dry-goods business is as strong as ever—so obviously somebody's still using them. Like in the war, nobody was making typewriters, but people kept on using them anyway. A little bit of maintenance and regular use and you can keep a typewriter running a long time. These other machines, computers and so on, even electric typewriters, they have a soul that's hooked into the wall. A manual typewriter has a soul that doesn't need anything else in order to exist—it exists in itself. People are always going to like that about a manual."

(1997)

SINK OR SWIM

This story begins in the New York Public Library on Forty-second Street. I was at the interlibrary-loan desk, filling out a form for a book I needed. The librarian saw my Brooklyn address, and he said, "Oh, you live in Park Slope. I live there, too." I finished with that and then went home and began to load the car. My wife and two-year-old daughter and I were going to visit friends in Vermont. I packed suitcases and toys and presents and books and fishing equipment—wherever we go, we take a lot of stuff. As I was loading, the sky became so dark that the streetlights came on, and all at once it began to pour. My wife and daughter and I set out in the rain. A block from our apartment, as I turned from Eighth Avenue onto Ninth Street, I noticed that torrents of rainwater were running down the street along both curbs. Park Slope does indeed slope, and at the bottom of Ninth, just past Second Avenue, the rainwater had accumulated into a big puddle. Actually, it was more like a lake. My wife said maybe I shouldn't drive into it, but the minute I hesitated, cars behind me honked. So I went ahead.

A city bus surged in front of me, leaving quite a wake. I followed it, and immediately, water came through the floor of the car. Then it came up to the seats. My wife and I were saying various things to each other. As the water began to come over the seats, the engine died. The cars behind me honked. Terrified that I might impede traffic, I leaped out into the waist-deep water. Old tires and forty-ounce malt-liquor bottles were bobbing around beside me. I began to push the car, which was not difficult, because it was floating. I could have pushed it with one hand. I waded, propelling the car before me, until I got it to drier land. Then the car became almost impossible to push. I had to wait for it to drain. The rain had stopped, so my wife got out and took our daughter and one or two suitcases, walked up the steps to the Smith Street station, and rode the F train two stops back to our apartment.

I called a garage in my neighborhood, and they sent a tow truck. The driver looked at the engine and said it was probably ruined (he was right—the car never really ran again, and I junked it soon after). Lots of local guys in low-slung shorts gathered around and joined in the autopsy.

The driver towed the car to the garage's lot and said they couldn't look at it until after the weekend. He said the lot was not very secure and that I shouldn't leave anything in the car. I somehow managed to load myself with all our stuff, and as I was walking up the sidewalk, a slow-moving heap of wet suitcases and shopping bags and stuffed animals and fishing rods, I saw coming toward me the librarian from interlibrary loans. I remember the look on his mild face— surprised recognition, changing to mystification tinged with distaste. He didn't ask, though, and I didn't explain. Silently, we both accepted the possibility that I was insane and agreed to overlook it. We had a brief conversation about when the book I had ordered might arrive. Then I walked on toward home.

(1999)

THE MORNINGS AFTER

From the suburb where I live in New Jersey, you can see the skyline of Manhattan. When it appears through the trees or beyond the edge of a hill, I find myself checking it and checking it again, to see if the World Trade towers still aren't there. What happened to them and to the people in them is unacceptable to the mind, and we must use a lot of effort to get it straight. To accommodate ourselves to the facts is to feel a weight that gets no lighter no matter how we adjust it. The weight has a particular heaviness in the early morning. After a troubled but forgetful sleep, I wake up at five forty-five, before first light. For a moment I don't remember what happened; in the next moment, fully awake, I do.

There's a kind of impact as memory revives: yes, what I'm remembering isn't a dreadful misgiving that ran through my sleep; it's real. Outside the bedroom, the morning is quiet. Traffic hasn't yet begun on the busy street in front of my house. As I lie there listening, I know that millions of my neighbors in the suburbs and the city are having the same experience I just had. People are waking; there's a heartbeat of not remembering, and then, heavily, memory returns. For me, pain of it is broad but not sharp, because no one close to me died in the attack. But for many thousands of survivors—the paper said hundreds of children lost a parent—the dawning memory is specific and hard and unrelieved, poking through the early morning like a piece of angle iron among the pillows.

I think of the weight of memory falling in all those houses and apartments in the quiet half hour or so before the day begins. It's a weight that's continental in size, and it has a motion, heading westward as people there start to wake up, too. The weight consists of details—orange and black explosions, news clips run over and over, the smoke from something that shouldn't burn, the headlong verticality of the buildings' gigantic collapse, a rush of history like the *Titanic* going down. Each detail produces its own inward wince. It's an unusual feeling, and not a bad one, to know that at a particular moment millions of your fellow citizens are all thinking about the same thing.

Of course, the mind doesn't exactly think about what happened. Rather, memories and images enter it unbidden, and it encounters them and veers away. For me, the attempts at evasion lead my thoughts to ridiculousness and fantasy. I remember the desperate image of people jumping from the building, and the next thing I know I'm thinking about what if some of them had happened to have hang gliders in their offices, and they launched themselves out the windows and came gliding safely down, hundreds of them gliding down and getting away. Or what if there'd been helicopters with big nets for people to jump into, or slurry bombers like they use in forest fires out west, and the slurry bombers swooped down into the Hudson and sucked up big loads of water and flew up over the towers and put out the fire?

Then my mind escapes even farther, the scenarios involving the brave people who decided to fight the terrorists on the plane that later crashed in western Pennsylvania. Lots of thoughts have taken refuge in them, I'm sure; they provided our only victory of the day. What they actually did was amazing enough. But what if those people (I daydream) had succeeded even more? What if they had not only attacked the terrorists but had subdued them, gotten control of the plane, and somehow landed it with all or most of the passengers still alive? Wouldn't that have been cool? If they had been able to do that, they would now be heroes such as America has never seen. Audie Murphy and Babe Ruth and the Founding Fathers themselves would shrink to nothing in comparison. We'd all be weeping and cheering still. The whole country would be at their feet, and the celebrities we pretend to be interested in for want of anyone better would disappear, possibly forever, in the brightness of the heroes' fame.

If I were really grieving, these daydreams would only make me feel worse in the long run. The farther you go from reality, the more it hurts when you come back. Plus I would probably hate myself for having such nugatory thoughts when someone I love had died. But my personal suffering, as it relates to this particular incident, is not the worst that humans have ever been through. In letters my grandmother wrote during World War II, she complained that due to wartime rationing she could not find nylons, cake mix, rubber overshoes, or crown rib roast in the stores; aside from a few travel inconveniences, I have not had to deal with difficulties even as small as hers. At the end of President Bush's speech laying out our country's response to the attack, he said that sacrifices would be asked of the American people. The first sacrifice he mentioned, as I recall, was "Hug your kids." I have hugged my kids a lot since then. Doing that has been no trouble.

Last spring I became kind of obsessed with Osama bin Laden. I had seen an FBI "Wanted" poster on the wall of a post office in a town near where I live, and I had studied that poster microscopically. Among the bin Laden facts that interested me was how really tall and skinny he was—possibly 6 foot 6, possibly 140 pounds, according to the FBI. I even wrote an article about my bin Laden musings and about "Wanted" posters in general. Driving on our local Jersey streets, my friend Bill and I would occasionally pass the time by ruling out pedestrians as possible bin Ladens in disguise: "Too short"; "Too fat"; "Too young"; "Too old." This idleness looked different later, when I learned that some of the September 11 attackers may have lived in the communities of Wayne and Fort Lee, both just a few miles away.

I don't know exactly why bin Laden interested me as he did. Maybe it was because so much back then seemed known—what the Republicans would say, what the Democrats would say; what the news would do with the next scandal; what one interest group would argue about another; what we all wanted, i.e., more. But there, on the post office wall, was someone peering out from the (to me) complete unknown. And not just unknown, but far away. That was part of the joke: how far bin Laden certainly was from his picture on the post office wall.

After the attack, at the very moment when we began to bomb Afghanistan, bin Laden released a videotape of himself saying that the destruction in America was an act of God's vengeance and threatening more violence to come. Everyone in the world saw it, so I don't have to describe the outdoor daylight he was sitting in, the rock outcropping behind him, the camouflage jacket (possibly of U.S. Army issue) he had on. People in America perhaps did not like to think how frightening it was to have this man's face pop up on their TV screens the second the cruise missiles flew, as if he'd been hiding back there all the time. The president's office, in a conference call, asked the five men in charge of most news broadcasts in this country not to show this video or others like it, and they agreed. The idea was to prevent the passing of encouragement or secret messages to the enemy. The deeper reason, of course, was that the video scared us.

If I could, I would watch this video many times. I want to listen to bin Laden's voice, not the translator's, until I can recognize it on the phone; I want to absorb his offhand manner, the half-lidded expression in his eyes, the enormity of his matter-of-fact acceptance of the loss of so many lives. Bin Laden is six years younger than I. In a generational sense, he's not unfamiliar; I seem to remember guys like him, even down to the turban and camo jacket, sitting at a table by themselves in the college dining hall. And yet as I watch him it's dizzying, overwhelming, to imagine the galactic distance between us. To me, he is a cartoon archvillain become horribly real. To him, I and three hundred million other Americans are instruments of Satan, and also fools.

Anyone who has been an American traveler in a poor foreign country knows how foolish you feel sometimes. As for how foolish you look, local people can always be found who will fill you in on that. Our optimism, childishness, naïveté, lack of guile, and belief in comfort and safety attract plenty of scorn. Equally bad, in critical foreign eyes, is our ability to disengage: when our fantasy of the world is punctured, we run back to our American homes and let the whole foreign experience evaporate like a dream.

Nobody can accuse us of being too isolated and safe anymore. What used to be far from us has become near, international war and large-scale religious hatred unfortunately included. Even if we still want to, we can't disengage as easily as we did before. Maybe our next struggle will be to remain our hopeful, foolish selves while enmeshed, now inextricably, in the wised-up world.

(2002)

BAGS IN TREES: A RETROSPECTIVE

For more than ten years now, I've been tangled up with the problem of plastic bags stuck in trees. If I've learned anything from the experience, it's "Be careful what you notice." I was living in Brooklyn; I noticed the many plastic bags flapping by their handles from the high branches of trees, cheerful and confident and out of reach. Noticing led to pondering, pondering led to an invention: the bag snagger, a prong-and-hook device that, when attached to a long pole, removes bags and other debris from trees with satisfying efficiency. My friend Tim McClelland made the first working model in his jewelry studio on Broome Street, downtown. Possessing the tool, we of course had to use it; we immediately set off on a sort of harvest festival of bag snagging.

Tim's older brother, Bill, came, too. With snagger and poles (interlocking ones, of aluminum, at first) stowed in Bill's Taurus, we snagged in every New York borough, sometimes going out twice a week. We found bags everywhere, by the thousand; the ultrafine traffic soot that collects on them covered our hands like graphite. Then our ambition led us farther, on bag-snagging jaunts to Massachusetts, Rhode Island, and New Jersey. From someone at a party I heard that trees along the Mississippi River were full of debris after the big floods of 1993, so one August we drove to the river and did a lot of snagging on both the Illinois and the Missouri sides. An environmental group invited us to come to Los Angeles and help with a cleanup along the Los Angeles River, so Bill and I flew out and snagged bags and debris from the prickly desert flora there. For a long while, bag snagging became our main outdoor recreation, completely obliterating the occasional mornings we'd formerly given to golf.

Bill and Tim and I are all transplanted Midwesterners. They grew up in Michigan, I in Ohio. Bill went to my high school in Ohio. We used to do some wild things. Get Tim to tell you about the time at his parents' house outside Rochester, Michigan, on New Year's Eve when he and I decided it would be a great idea to shoot a flashlight out of a tree from a moving toboggan. We tied the flashlight to a branch above a toboggan run on their property, and we were sitting on the toboggan, Tim in front, me in back, me with a loaded shotgun, both of us scooching with our heels to get the toboggan started, when Bill and his (now) wife, Jean, intervened.

Or another time, this one in my loft in lower Manhattan: Tim and I were sitting around drinking Jack Daniel's and beer, and we took my twenty-gauge shotgun down and started fooling with it. Tim asked if I had any ammo for it, and I said I did, and I went and got it. He asked how you loaded it, and I chambered a shell. It happened that my girlfriend (now wife) had moved out a few weeks earlier. Not long before she left, she had persuaded me, at the cost of much labor and hauling by ropes up the elevator shaft, to add a heavy oak bookshelf to our few loft furnishings. I had never figured out where to put the bookshelf, and it still stood in the middle of the floor at one end of the loft, about forty feet from where Tim and I were sitting. The bookshelf had a back of particle board. Hefting the gun, I looked at the shelf for a while, and listened to determine if my neighbors upstairs and down were home; the floor and ceiling in that loft were thin enough so that I could usually hear my neighbors moving around. Nobody home, I decided. I stood, aimed at the bookshelf, and fired. The sound of a shotgun in a brick-walled, enclosed space like that is indescribably loud. There was also the skittery sound of the birdshot pellets going across the floor on the other side of the big hole they blew in the particle board. I don't think Tim or I had ever laughed that hard.

Blue gun smoke filled the room. I gave the gun to Tim, and he aimed and pulled the trigger. We laughed even harder at this explosion, because now we knew better what to expect. I took the gun and fired again. A thick fog of gun smoke hung everywhere. Just then the buzzer rang. It was Bill and two friends. They came in, saw the gun smoke, saw the empty bottle and beer cans on the floor, saw the spent shells, and heard us babbling. They began to back out the door. Amazingly, though, we were able to persuade them that taking a shot would be really fun, and eventually all three of them (one a pacifist woman nurse) did.

Maybe because we grew up surrounded by space and

horizons and long views, we Midwesterners felt confined in the city, or constrained. Sometimes we talked about how cool it would be to see a cargo plane at ten thousand feet drop dozens of yellow Checker cabs over an empty area like the Sheep Meadow in Central Park, and how the taxis would look falling into the city against the blue of the sky; or how cool it would be to get a bucket of golf balls and hit them, one after the next, up Fifth Avenue some deserted Sunday morning. That last fantasy we partially enacted, buying range balls by the gross and hitting them into the East and Hudson rivers from the lower Manhattan shoreline. Stroking a long, soaring drive and bouncing it off a support beam of the Manhattan Bridge gave a deeply pleasurable sensation that began in the shoulders and spread down the spine to the toes.

For us, bag snagging represented a more socialized form of the fun we'd been having, or imagining, before. Snagging gave the thrill of vandalism yet was its opposite—mischievous good, rather than mischievous bad. During our bag-snagging foray along the Mississippi, a woman photographer who accompanied us (I was writing about the adventure for *Outside* magazine) looked at us in puzzlement, trying to get a grasp on our hard-to-explain hobby. Then she asked, "Is this bag snagging part of a twelve-step program, or something, that you guys are involved in?" The question made us stop for a moment. She wasn't right, yet her intuition hadn't been entirely wrong.

It goes without saying that the city was different then. Lower Manhattan, with its tendency to depopulate on weekends, was our favorite bagging ground; we used to take stuff out of trees in public spaces that are closely patrolled or completely fenced off (or nonexistent) now. We even had our own traffic cone, with which we redirected traffic when we wanted to work on a branch overhanging the street. Once or twice, we walked unauthorized and unescorted through private buildings to get to a high entanglement that could be reached only from an inner courtyard. People assumed we had some kind of official status, when in fact we had no status at all.

Only once were we seriously challenged. Tim and I had spent a Saturday afternoon among the London plane trees in the lawn around City Hall, experimenting with the aluminum poles at the greatest extension we had yet tried, forty-five or fifty feet. At that length, the pole tends to bend not just over but back again, in a noodly sine curve that makes it difficult to control. As we were trying to master it, a white Parks Department pickup jerked to a stop on a nearby piece of pavement, and a fierce, burly Parks Department guy named Dave Miller hopped out. He asked us what we were doing, and when we tried to explain cut us off with the information that we were breaking the law and that if we injured the trees we could be fined or jailed.

Again we explained, and a grudging curiosity got the better of him. High in one of the plane trees nearby, beyond the reach of anything but a cherry picker, a large plastic drop cloth had wrapped itself around a crotch of boughs. Rashly, we offered to take it out while he observed. We had never before snagged anything that high. Dave Miller hesitated, then gave his permission and stood back, arms folded, a scowl on his heavy brow. Tim tried for a while and budged the drop cloth without freeing it. My heart was pounding as if we were auditioning on Broadway. As I watched, I realized that the plastic was in a simple knot that it could be backed out of. I took over, put the wobbly pole on the target, pushed and turned the plastic, unknotted it from the tree crotch, and lowered it to the lawn on the end of the pole like a captured standard. Dave Miller all but leaped for joy. He had a passerby photograph him with us, the pole, and the drop cloth, he shook our hands twice, and on the spot he issued us official Parks Department volunteer cards.

Eventually, we removed drop cloths by the dozen. In Manhattan, they are a common kind of high-branch entanglement. They fall into trees from skyscrapers under construction and other upper-story sites. Tarps, also—you get a lot of them, especially around bridges. From two trees under the Williamsburg Bridge, Bill and Tim removed an immense blue canvas tarp complete with grommets. Evidently it had blown off the back of a truck and landed on the trees, smothering and oppressing them like an incubus. In fact, a lot of what ends up in Manhattan's trees falls into them or is thrown. People get mad and chuck other people's stuff out the window. Sometimes as we removed a series of objects— Walkman, T-shirt, sneakers, underpants, pajama bottoms— we understood that they had all once been the possessions of the same unfortunate guy.

Of course, the basic thing that gets in a New York City tree is the white plastic deli bag. It reaches the tree with the aid of the wind, or (as I sometimes think) by its own power.

With its filmy whiteness and its two looped handles, it suggests a self-levitating undershirt; we have named it the undershirt bag. It does not have a soul, but it imitates one, rising and floating on the exhalations of a subway grate like the disembodied spirits that poets used to converse with in Hell. Its prehensile handles cling to any branch that comes within range, and then grab hold for eternity. This bag is not hard to get out of a tree when it's still fresh, but as it ages and shreds it becomes more difficult. The plastic dry-cleaning bag is its sinister companion. After only a day or two of windshredding, the micron-thick plastic of a dry-cleaning bag is all but unremovable. Almost as common as either of those are audiotape and videotape. We have removed furlongs of both, and Bill (who's a composer) has carefully spliced some of the fragments piece to piece; the result, when played, resembles a door suddenly opened on a hall of howling, tedious demons.

If you spend a lot of time taking bags out of trees, you learn that they don't wish anybody well. It's no accident that a visual convention for spookiness is dangling spiderwebs, moss-draped branches, jungly, heart-of-darkness drooping vines. Though not the Dark Power itself, bags in trees nonetheless act as its minions; or, to put it another way, nothing makes a neighborhood look scarier than barebranch trees draped with plastic-bag shreds above a razor-wire fence similarly fluttering and bestrewn. The bags and debris are an established part of the picture. They like it up there and prefer not to be disturbed.

Once, at a pedestrian mall between Roosevelt Avenue

and Union Street in Queens, Tim and I were taking detritus out of some young linden trees growing in pots. The trees had been afflicted, years before, with a bondage of little holiday lights in strings. The lights had long ago quit working and had been abandoned rather than taken down. We were pretty sure they had no current anymore, but getting electrocuted via our aluminum poles was still a concern. I began on one tree and Tim on another, twenty yards or so away.

I noticed a dirty blue bath towel hanging between some branches. It seemed to bulge a bit; I figured it was full of water, as is a lot of trash in trees. With the hook of the snagger, I cut the bulge to drain it. Instantly a large rat sprang from the hole I'd made and shot down the pole at me. I remember seeing its teeth. It moved so fast it would have reached my hands before I let go of the pole, but at the last split second it leaped from the pole to another tree, scrabbled swiftly up, leaped to the roof of a building, and disappeared.

Even onlooking pigeons sometimes got upset with us and wanted us to leave well enough alone. As we wielded our pole, they would fly at us with keening, gurgling cries. In Collect Pond Park, on Centre Street downtown, we were trying to remove a pigeon that had caught its foot in a piece of party balloon wrapped around a high branch—that ribbon is like wire, and the pigeon, unable to free itself, had died—and as we were maneuvering the pole closer suddenly all the park's many pigeons began swooping near the corpse protectively and diving toward our heads. Soon a riot of pigeons filled the high, narrow shaft formed by the gloomy government buildings looming around. We ended up leaving the body where it was.

Among the city's human occupants, a few seemed to like what we were doing. Now and then, windows in an apartment building overlooking a tree we were debagging would go up, and a resident would lean out and applaud. A nice elderly lady might call down and invite us in for a tuna sandwich and a glass of grape juice; an old man once thanked me and gave me a dollar. Or else people said things to us like, "Thank God the city is finally doing something about this problem." Other observers, naturally, heckled us and told us we were idiots. By the Walt Whitman housing projects, in Brooklyn, someone dropped a forty-ounce beer bottle from an upper window to a point on the lawn uncomfortably near us. When I tried to describe bag snagging to some black and Latino students in a class I visited at Kingsborough Community College, a lot of them were offended that anyone could devote time to an activity so (to them) pointless and unnecessary.

At home, the reaction of our wives to our newfound pastime was what Alice Kramden's would have been to a similar scheme of Ralph's. This reaction grew more pronounced during the period when some of the objects we removed from trees seemed so interesting to us that we began bringing them home. I got a sense of the opinion of wives in general one afternoon when I'd spent the day indoors with domestic duties and took a break by doing some snagging on my own in Prospect Park and vicinity. When I came back, our downstairs neighbor, Chris Avanzino, happened to be standing on the stoop, her baby on her hip. She looked me over and said, "Your wife is in there taking care of your two-year-old kid with a hundred-and-two-degree temperature and you're walking around the neighborhood with a *pole* taking bags out of *trees* . . ." She shook her head and gave me a pitying, soul-withering smile.

Our pursuit of bag snagging led down various paths—for example, into the obscurities of patent law. Tim and I thought our snagger might be patentable, because probably no device like it had ever existed before. Our first patent attorney, a calm, bald man named Charlie Blank, said he thought our chances of getting a patent were good. Then he retired. Another attorney at Charlie Blank's firm took over our application, and a year or two later told us that the Patent and Trademark Office had rejected it because a fruit picker patented in 1869 duplicated our snagger's function— something to do with a similar hook on the end of the fruit picker. Our attorney appealed the decision, on the grounds that the fruit picker would not work as effectively on plastic bags, which in any event did not exist back in 1869. This time, the patent office agreed and issued us U.S. Patent No. 5,566,538. *The New York Times* selected our snagger for mention in its weekly "Patents" column, along with a surgical tool that uses a tiny beam of water moving at supersonic speed to cut human eye tissue. We were delighted to get the patent—it's like a small asterisk of immortality.

Partly because of the patent, and through a set of other circumstances too complicated to go into, I appeared in a movie, *Blue in the Face* (Miramax, 1995, starring Harvey Keitel), in a cameo role as myself talking about bags in trees. The movie did not do very well. In the art theater where I saw it, I was the only person in the audience. The host of a radio show in New York happened to see the movie, however, and he asked Bill and Tim and me to be on his show. The husband of Bette Midler, the singer and movie star, heard the broadcast and afterward called the radio station and asked if we would sell him a bag snagger as a birthday present for his wife. Bette Midler, as people know, is an enemy of litter, and she shares our opinion of bags in trees. Bette Midler liked the snagger her husband gave her and eventually she bought more of them for the cleanup crew she sponsors in the city, and the hardworking kids who staff it began to make a real dent in uptown bags in trees.

With the hope of selling a lot more bag snaggers, we formed a company, Bag Snaggers, Inc. A man in California who has a small business manufacturing and selling specialty poles—tree-pruning poles, snake-lassoing poles, monkey-catching poles for use in airplane cargo hangars when monkeys escape from shipping crates and climb up into the rafters—agreed to manufacture our snagger and interlocking fiberglass poles to go with it. We listed ourselves in some public-works Web sites and catalogs, and sold a few sets to civic groups and municipalities. Bill, who handled the paperwork, began referring to Bag Snaggers, Inc., as a "multi-hundred-dollar company." But, over time, our sales were not brisk. The park employees and groundskeepers of America evidently are not keen on shelling out for a tool that will involve them in new duties wrangling debris out of trees. Recently, Bill and Tim and I have been talking about dissolving the company and shutting operations down.

The truth is, these days we don't go bag snagging as much as we used to. None of us live in the city anymore; Tim moved his jewelry business to Great Barrington, Massachusetts, I moved to Montana and then New Jersey, and Bill was in New Jersey all along. We have families and the usual excess of more important obligations. A morning of bag snagging requires logistics and scheduling and phone calls. Plus, when we started doing this we were younger; reaching sixty feet of wobbly fiberglass into a tree and snagging a bag amid obstructing branches can be vexingly hard. We've begun to get bag-snagging injuries—shoulder, neck, back—and around the house the sympathy available for them is only the negative kind. We hoped that a new group of young guys would see the appeal of our tree-bag pursuit and take over, but so far that hasn't happened. Apparently, bag-snagging fever was specific just to us, and just to then.

Stuff having to do with bag snagging still comes up. People think of bags in trees, and they think of us. An aid worker just back from Africa tells us that there's a lot of debris in trees in the poorer parts of Africa, and the closer you get to the supposed epicenter of the AIDS epidemic the more of it there is. An Irishwoman says that in Ireland bags in trees are called "witches' knickers." A resident of the Upper East Side writes to tell us that ever since some balloons got stuck in a tree outside her bedroom window her family has had bad luck with health; she asks if we can take the balloons out, and one afternoon we do. We still accept special requests occasionally.

At a midtown cocktail party a while ago, Thomas Mallon, the novelist, asked me if we still took bags out of trees. I said we did, and he said he had a related problem: helium-filled Mylar balloons that float to the ceiling of Grand Central Station and linger there for months. He asked if there was anything we could do about this. I said I would check it out.

The next time I was in Grand Central, I saw what he meant. The vaulted ceiling of the main concourse rises a hundred feet or more above the station's marble floor. The height is lofty but still measurable in human terms—it's the heart-stopping altitude of the tightrope walker, the altitude of prophetic ascension and rocket liftoff. When visitors come into the station for the first time, their eyes go to the ceiling, and, in the vast interior space the ceiling encloses, their prospects seem to expand. Looking up in Grand Central evokes feelings of vertigo and excitement and fear of heights and dizziness and exaltation that may recall the reasons you moved to New York City in the first place. The ceiling is the dark greenish-blue of a clear summer-night sky, studded with small lights representing stars in the constellations of the zodiac, with the figures of the zodiac outlined in off-white around them. And there in the middle of the ceiling—in the constellation of Pisces—was a shiny, silver, heart-shaped Mylar balloon.

I came back week after week and kept tabs on it. It moved only slightly, between the ventral fins of one of Pisces's fish. Once, I was there in July and a tour guide leading a group said in annoyance that the balloon had been up there since Valentine's Day. A Metro-North worker standing by a track entrance said that tourists had just complained to him about the balloon ruining their photographs. By then, thousands or millions of Grand Central passersby must have seen it. In this most public of American public spaces, the balloon was unreachable, top of the world, thumb in your eye.

Obviously we could not get to it with bag-snagging poles. Even if we braced the poles with some kind of tripod, the ceiling is too high. From a guy who works for the Bryant Park conservancy, Bill heard that a cook from the Oyster Bar restaurant, on the lower level of the station, used to shoot balloons down at night with a BB gun when he got off work, but to me shooting seemed too much of a risk to the recently restored zodiac paintings, as well as not quite sporting, somehow. And then there are the Homeland Security soldiers who patrol the station with their M-16s . . .

So we thought about it, and here's the idea: get three other helium balloons at a florist's or party store; cover the balloons with double-sided tape, judiciously, so as not to affect their buoyancy; tie the tape-covered balloons to stout monofilament line on a fishing rod; stand beneath the balloon lodged on the ceiling; send the retriever balloons aloft until they touch the other balloon; nudge them around until the tape adheres; then reel the retrievers and their tape-stuck captive back down.

Recently, Bill and I ran a field test of this idea under a tall highway bridge in the Jersey Meadowlands. First, we sent up a target balloon on a long lead. It came to a stop between two girders. Then we sent the retrievers. Despite a brisk wind (which, of course, would be absent in Grand Central), the retriever balloons reached the target balloon, nestled around it with a kind of natural gregariousness, stuck to it with the double-sided tape, and held it securely enough so that we could reel them and it down. Repeated tests achieved the same result. Man, the toolmaker: at our success, the marshy New Jersey landscape stretched around us in submission, like background scenery in a portrait of Sir Isaac Newton. This idea can work, we are 100 percent sure. Whenever we get the go-ahead from the company that manages Grand Central, we're ready.

(2004)

ROUTE 3

Between me in a New Jersey suburb and New York City, fifteen-some miles to the east, runs a highway called Route 3. For many bus and car commuters, it is essentially the only direct road from here (and other suburbs) to there. To say that billions of vehicles use it daily is an exaggeration, traffic experts will tell you. People have written songs about the fabled Route 66, and the phrase "New Jersey Turnpike" has a metrical neatness that fits it into certain rock-and-roll tunes; but as far as I know nobody has sung about Route 3. Its unavoidable, traffic-packed, unalluring, grimly lifelike quality defeats the lyric impulse, probably. Route 3 starts on the low north-south New Jersey ridges where many suburbs are, crosses the miles-wide swamp that developers started referring to as the Meadowlands some years ago, rises to another ridge near the Hudson River, and joins an artery bringing an accumulation of traffic down the spinning drain into the Lincoln Tunnel and, at the other end, the vast retort of Manhattan.

An eastbound traveler on Route 3 sometimes has the serrated skyline of Midtown straight ahead. At certain times of the year during the morning commute, the sun comes up right behind the city; the shadows of the buildings theoretically stretch the whole length of the highway and slide backward gradually, like tide. When the road reaches the Meadowlands, the sky opens out, with the tall light poles of the Giants Stadium parking lot receding to a remote vanishing point and the pools of swamp water perfectly reflecting the reeds along their edges, the radio towers, the clouds, and the intricate undersides of cautious airplanes descending to Newark Airport. Along much of the road on either side, the landscape is as ordinary as ordinary America can be: conventioneers' hotels and discount stores and fast-food restaurants and office complexes and Home Depot and Best Buy and Ethan Allen, most of the buildings long and low, distributed in the spread-out style of American highway architecture. And then suddenly, just before the Lincoln Tunnel, that ordinariness ends, and you're in jostling, close-up surroundings about to become New York. At no other entry to the city is the transition between it and everyday, anywhere U.S.A. so quick.

I usually travel to and from the city by bus. The one I take to go home leaves from the fourth floor of the Port Authority Bus Terminal. Most bus commuters sensibly occupy themselves with newspapers, laptops, CD players, and so on. I always try to get a window seat and then look at the scenery. If this were a ride at an amusement park, I would pay to go on it. The bus comes out of the terminal on a high ramp above Ninth Avenue. For just a moment you can see clear down Ninth, a deep ravine usually filled at the bottom with taxicabs. From the ramp, the bus descends into the tunnel, either straight or in a loop, depending on traffic and time of day. Once in the tunnel, it can be there forever. Brake lights on vehicles ahead reflect on the bus ceiling and tint people's faces. During an evening rush hour, my son and I observed a foot sticking up from the narrow electric tram cart that runs on a track along the tunnel wall. The foot had on a work boot and the shin was wearing work pants. We decided that it must belong to a tunnel worker who was out of sight down in the cart taking a nap.

When the bus leaves the tunnel, it is in Weehawken, New Jersey. It climbs the elevated spiral of highway that people call the helix, and then for a mile or so there's a complicated section of road where traffic bound in different directions sorts itself out. Then the bus turns northwest onto Route 3. At this point, it is in Secaucus. A newspaper story some years ago said that state police had seized about a ton and a quarter of cocaine in a truck just as it left a warehouse in Secaucus off Route 3. I'm not sure which warehouse it was, but I have some likely ones in mind. Route 3 in Secaucus is where the transition to ordinary America occurs; prominent on your right are two large signs that say "Royal Motel."

What fixed the Royal Motel in my mind, and what makes me glad, somehow, every time I pass it, was a story that appeared in the *Daily News* in 2000. The story said that one morning, at 2:13 a.m., New York City police arrested a woman for soliciting prostitution at the corner of Tenth Avenue and Forty-sixth Street. The woman gave her name as Tacoma Hopps. The police handcuffed her, put her in the back of a Ford minivan they were using to transport suspects, and left her there while they went to make another arrest. Tacoma Hopps squeezed her hands through the hand-cuffs, got in the van's driver seat, and sped off downtown. Before the police, suddenly left afoot, could radio ahead to stop her, she had driven to the tunnel and through it. She then left the vehicle in Secaucus and began walking along Route 3, barefoot and carrying a green duffel bag. Secaucus police spotted her. In the duffel bag were two bulletproof vests, a pistol clip containing twenty-five hollow-point bullets, and a New York City Police radio, parking permit, and vehicle keys. When the New York police arrested her, she had given her home address as the Royal Motel. When the Secaucus police arrested her, that was apparently where she was going.

Beyond Secaucus, the bus crosses the wide Hackensack River; the fact that there are no other vehicle bridges over the Hackensack for miles upstream and down contributes to Route 3's congestion. West of the river, on the bus's right, you see the Continental Airlines Arena and Giants Stadium. Recently, developers announced that behind the stadium they're going to build a 104-acre recreation complex, with indoor ski slopes and a surfing pool, to be called Xanadu. Beyond the stadium is swamp and another big river, the Passaic. Then come hills and houses, and trees instead of reeds. In some places here, the road's shoulders glitter with a boa of trash; in others, the right lane merges almost undetectably with large, vague parking lots around commercial enterprises. One of these is the Tick Tock Diner, a chrome Art Deco structure outlined in four colors of neon and surmounted by clocks. When Sean J. Richard, a labor racketeer associated with New Jersey's DeCavalcante family, heard a while back that he was to meet with a capo (alleged) from

New York's Lucchese family named Dominic Truscello in a van outside the Tick Tock Diner, Mr. Richard became so frightened that he soon decided to turn state's evidence. His testimony is expected to put a few people in jail.

Across from the Tick Tock, the 127-acre factory and laboratory compound of Hoffmann–La Roche Pharmaceuticals rises in buildings of utopian whiteness, one upon the next. On the top of the highest building is the lighted logo of the company—"ROCHE," inside a capsule-shaped border. Valium, the company's famous sedative, introduced in 1963, earned a lot of the money that built this Acropolis of pharmaceuticals. Anxiety sufferers of that era probably remember the Valium pill. It was small and round, of a color between yellow and white. On one side a thin, fine score divided the pill into halves; on the other was the word "ROCHE" and beneath it the number 5 (meaning milligrams). A friend who works as a statistician for the company tells me that although the formula for Valium went out of patent a long time ago and cheaper versions exist, the company still sells a lot of it. Evidently, the name and the look of the Roche pill have acquired a magic that transcends chemistry. Leo H. Sternbach, Valium's inventor, is ninety-five years old and lives not far from me. My friend says that when Mr. Sternbach stops by the lab, as he still occasionally does, he is treated like a king.

Past Hoffmann–La Roche on the same side of the street, at the top of a hill with a lawn, the Holy Face Monastery sits half out of sight behind trees. At the foot of the driveway, right beside Route 3, the monastery has erected a shrine. It is a statue of Jesus on a white brick pedestal with concrete tablets nearby bearing the Ten Commandments. Jesus' arms are raised as if in benediction of the traffic; the position of one hand is such that a beer can just fits in it, a coincidence that jokesters take advantage of. I have often seen people, usually alone, praying before the shrine in the mornings and later in the day. They stand with heads bared and bowed and hands clasped at their waists, sometimes so deep in prayer that they seem to be in another dimension.

Now the bus turns off Route 3 at the Grove Street, Montclair/Paterson exit. It proceeds along Grove, stopping occasionally to let passengers out. When it pulls over, the branches of trees along the street brush the bus's top and side. To a suburbanite just come from the city, the scratching of branches and leaves on metal is the sound of being home.

As a grown-up, I have lived in Manhattan, Brooklyn, and Montana. Now I live in the New Jersey town of Montclair. Recently, a friend who's a rancher in Wyoming sent me a card saying he finds it hard to believe that he has a friend who lives in New Jersey. Sometimes I find it hard to believe I'm here, myself. When I lived in the city, I had the usual New Yorker's disdain for this state. Oddly, though, I was attracted to it, too. I used to come over to Jersey a lot, maybe because it reminded me of Ohio and other places I love in the middle of the country. I like being on the continent, rather than slightly offshore. I get a sense that I'm more connected to it; when there's a big snowstorm, for example, I imagine the snow stretching from here back across the Alleghenies to Ohio in unbroken white. And I like the feeling that I'm near the city but also just out of its range.

Suburban New Jersey is a bunch of different stuff mixed up like a garage sale. George Washington kept his army in this area throughout a year of the Revolutionary War; the British held the city, and he wanted to be close to it yet strategically hard for them to get to. His ally the Marquis de Lafayette stayed in a farmhouse on Valley Road in Upper Montclair. A local chapter of the DAR has preserved the farmhouse's flat stone doorstep near the spot where the house was. The memorial, with the stone, a small plaque, and a flagpole, is in a little niche in the town's business district. On one side of the niche is a photo-finishing-and-retouching store, on the other a place called the Backrub Shoppe (recently closed), which offered back rubs lasting from ten minutes up to an hour.

On long walks through suburbs whose names I sometimes can't keep straight—Glen Ridge, Bloomfield, Brookside, Nutley, Passaic, Garfield, Lodi, Hasbrouck Heights, Hackensack, Teaneck, Leonia—I've encountered the New Jersey miscellany up close. Giant oil tanks cluster below expensive houses surrounded by hedges not far from abandoned factories with high brick smokestacks; a Spanish-speaking store that sells live chickens is near a Polish nightclub off a teeming eight-lane highway; a Greek church on a festival day roasts goats in fifty-five-gallon drums in its parking lot down the road from tall white Presbyterian churches that were built when everything around was countryside. Neighborhoods go from fancy to industrial to shabby without apparent reason, and you can't predict what the next corner will be.

From a car on a highway, though, suburban New Jersey looks so nondescript and ordinary as to be invisible. The eye, in passing, registers not this specific place but a generic likeness that has reproduced itself all across the country. In the Montclair Art Museum is a room of landscape paintings by the artist George Inness, who lived in Montclair from 1885 to 1894. They show the land before it was developed and paved. Inness's winter-gray hilltop tree lines, his ridges sloping underfoot, and his high sky lit by the presence of the ocean over the horizon are all still here, somewhere among the roads and buildings and wires now obscuring them.

That invisibility may explain, partly, why commuters on the bus don't bother to look out the window: everything there has been seen and reseen and accounted for until it might as well be a blank wall. The only people who regularly look out the bus window are young children. Except during traffic delays, the one time the adult passengers all sit up and stare out en masse is when the bus is driven by a man named Sal. Sal is short and has a boyish (though graying) shock of hair. His movements are more antic than usual for a bus driver. Sal is the only bus driver I know of who seems to notice what's along the road. When he sees something that interests him, he takes up the microphone and announces it to the passengers. Colorful Halloween displays, Christmas lights, a yard full of yellow and purple crocuses, the Goodyear blimp over Giants Stadium—all rate an excited mention by Sal, followed by his usual exclamation: "Oh-boy-oh-boy-oh-boy-oh-boy!"

When the bus gets to the Port Authority and is going up the ramp, Sal always says, "Ladies and gentlemen, boys and girls, I'd like to welcome you to the beautiful Caribbean island of Aruba"—or St. Martin, Barbuda, St. Thomas, etc.— "where the temperature is a sunny seventy-eight degrees.

Complimentary beverages will be served upon arrival, don't forget to put on your sunblock, and have a happy day! Cha-cha-cha!" Inside the terminal, when he opens the bus door in the line of buses that are disembarking passengers, he says, "Ahh, smell that fresh Caribbean air!"

For a while after September 11, Sal quit doing his announcements. His bus pulled into the station in silence, with the passengers waiting expectantly but in vain. The loss of Sal's announcements, minor as it was, saddened me out of proportion. Without some silliness, what is life for? Later, though, to general relief, Sal went back to giving what he calls his "spiels."

Although I shouldn't, I often let New Jersey traffic get to me. When I drive here, I am often beeped at for coming to a complete stop at stop signs, not running yellow lights, yielding the right of way at intersections, and following other rules of the road that local practice has discarded. At each beep, I jump and swear. After the relatively easygoing traffic of Montana, New Jersey driving had a predatory fierceness I wasn't ready for. Also, not long after we moved, a man in Englewood was run over and killed in a Starbucks while sitting at a table near the window and working on his laptop. That increased my fears.

New Jersey is the fourth-smallest state in the country and the most densely populated. Especially in areas where traffic is at its worst, room for new roads can't be found. About five and a half million people in New Jersey have driver's licenses, and they drive more than seven million registered vehicles. Traffic planners sometimes mention tepid-sounding solutions like new toll systems to encourage off-peak travel or high-tech ways of alerting drivers to jams.

In fact, the main method for dealing with so many cars in so small a space is the traditional one of ad hoc free-for-all. A few years ago, in a survey of New Jersey drivers done by the Insurance Council of New Jersey and the state's AAA, 52 percent said that they are very angry or moderately angry when they drive. About 40 percent admitted that they are likely to curse or make gestures at other drivers, or to use their vehicles to punish them by tailgating, flashing high beams, slowing down to block them in a lane, etc.

The morning rush hour into the city has been getting earlier every year, newspapers say. It used to begin between six o'clock and seven, and now begins between five and six. Nearly a million vehicles cross into Manhattan from various directions every day. The *Daily News* says that if a similar number of vehicles were lined up single file they would stretch from New York City to Los Angeles. And yet no New Jersey highway is among the worst ten places for traffic congestion in the nation, as drivers in Atlanta or Seattle or Los Angeles can testify. To further add to Route 3's averageness, the traffic on it is not much different from traffic anywhere.

Recently, I decided to walk to the city along Route 3. Observing scenery makes me imagine going out in it, and I wanted to see the road other than through glass. From the bus, walking on the shoulder appeared to be possible. Twelve miles from the Grove Street exit to the Lincoln Tunnel did not seem far, and once there I would take the Weehawken ferry, because the tunnel does not have a walkway open to pedestrians. I hadn't been on a long ramble for a while. I put on broken-in shoes and brought a map, in case I had to detour. At about noon of a mild day in late fall, I set out.

From the railing of the Grove Street bridge, Route 3 curved out of sight to the east amid a dwindling succession of multiarmed towers carrying high-tension lines. At this off-peak hour, the road was, as usual, full of cars going fast. I chose the right-hand, eastbound lanes, because that side seemed to have more room. I came down the ramp, along the margin. Of course there was no sidewalk, but neither were there signs forbidding pedestrians. I passed the Holy Face Monastery and shrine. The shoulder was so irregular that I had to keep climbing over the guardrail and back again and tromping through weeds. The traffic blew by, thrumming with the dull rubber thumps of tires hitting pavement seams.

The earth beside this kind of highway is like no earth that ever was. Neither cultivated nor natural, it's beside the point, completely unnoticed, and slightly blurred from being passed so often and so fast. And yet plants still grow in it, luxuriantly—ailanthus, and sumac, and milkweed, and lots of others that know how to accommodate themselves to us. In the swampy parts, the common reed would take over the roadway in a blink if the traffic stopped.

The tangled brush and the reeds collect an omnium-gatherum of trash. I saw broken CDs, hubcaps, coils of wire, patient-consent forms for various acupuncture procedures, pieces of aluminum siding, fragments of chrome, shards of safety glass, Dunkin' Donuts coffee cups, condom wrappers, knocked-over road signs, burned-out highway flares, a high-lighter pen, a surgical glove, nameless pieces of discarded rusty machinery, a yellow rain slicker with "Macy's Studio" on the back . . . Scattered through the grass and weeds for miles were large, bright-colored plastic sequins. I knew where they had come from. Once, while on the bus, I saw a parade float—probably from the Puerto Rican Day Parade, held in the city—pull up alongside and then speed by. A car must have been towing it, though I don't remember the car. The float was going at least seventy, shimmying and wobbling, banners flapping, and these sequins were blowing off it in handfuls and billowing behind.

Sometimes, walking beside Route 3 got to be too much, owing to the narrowness of the shoulder or the thickness of the undergrowth, and then I would cut over to one or another smaller road nearby. In the Meadowlands, there are some noplace avenues you might expect to find in a Florida swamp where the developers have given up; on an access-type road, an eight-story office building of Smith Barney stands all by itself in the reeds. Farther on, Route 3 has the aspect of a parkway, running through expanses of grass that are easy to stroll across. Nothing occupies this short-grass region but occasional Canada geese keeping one eye on the traffic, like bartenders watching a drunk.

The challenging part of my journey would be crossing the Hackensack River. I had two choices, the westbound bridge or the eastbound bridge. Both are narrow and lack walkways, though they do have little ledges like wide curbs at the sides where a walkway should be. The westbound bridge offered the safety advantage of traffic coming at me rather than from behind; at that proximity to cars, however, it's better not to see. Also, the westbound bridge is a half mile long, and its railing is not high. I whacked through the reeds in the median to the eastbound bridge. It is shorter, because the river here is narrower. Here, at least, the bridge's other side was in sight. I put on the Macy's Studio slicker for increased visibility and started across. Walking on the curb ledge required a one-foot-in-front-of-the-other gait as the trucks and cars went by at sixty-five mph an arm's length away. I held the gritty railing with my right hand. Below, the brown Hackensack swirled around the wooden pilings of a former bridge. In these narrow confines, the traffic noise was a top-volume roar. After a long several minutes, I made it to the other side.

From there my way became complicated—now on Route 3, now detouring around an impassable part, now backtracking after a shoulder I'd been following dead-ended at a fence. In no-man's regions I sometimes found foot trails leading through the grass, but no clue about who had made them. By sunset, I was walking up a sloping sidewalk in Union City above approach lanes for the tunnel, and going faster than the traffic inbound. I went down to Boulevard East, turned onto a lane under the elevated span, crossed a road running along the river, and sat down to rest on a bench in a little waterfront park. Across the river was a recompense for five hours of walking: the city, its lights diffusing in the mist of faint clouds above it, the whole varied sequence of glittering buildings cropped ruler-straight at the bottom by the Hudson's dark waterline.

I walked to the ferry, paid five dollars for a ticket, got on, and in six minutes crossed to the pier at Thirty-eighth

Street. At the Port Authority, I caught a six-thirty bus, wedging myself in the very back row among four other middle-aged guys. The one next to me had a high forehead and a loosened tie. He was fooling with his laptop, and as the bus came through the tunnel he put on a DVD of a Bruce Springsteen concert and began to listen to it with earphones. He had it turned up so loud that the rest of us could hear, and he occasionally hummed tone-deafly along. We could have objected—but we were in New Jersey and it was Bruce, after all. The backseat, and the whole bus, with its closed-in, comfortably crowded atmosphere of people going home, seemed without any connection at all to the highway howling inaudibly just outside.

That night, I was shook up and couldn't sleep—as if walking beside so much noise and speed had rearranged my molecules. I thought of the commuter buses nose-to-tail in line for the tunnel, and the mass of idling cars converging. To live by the internal-combustion engine is to live on top of fire; a cyclone of explosions carries us along.

Aaron Burr and Alexander Hamilton fought their famous duel on the New Jersey side of the Hudson River, in the town of Weehawken, two hundred years ago this July. Aside from the construction of the Lincoln Tunnel, the duel is the biggest thing that ever happened in Weehawken or nearby. The town is not large, and the tunnel's toll plaza and approaches take up a lot of it; sometimes as the bus climbs through Weehawken I wonder if the duel site might be close, or even under the wheels. History books say the duel was held "on the Weehawken duelling grounds," which sounds specific. When I called the Weehawken Public Library and asked the librarian if she knew where the site was, she immediately referred me to the town's expert on local history, Edward A. Fleckenstein.

Mr. Fleckenstein lives atop the Weehawken cliff, in a house with a view across the Hudson River and straight down Forty-second Street. He kindly agreed to see me and met me at the door with his brother George. Both men are taller than average, hale, genial, and formal; though it was a Saturday morning, both had on jackets and ties. Edward is a semiretired attorney specializing in estates and corporate law, and George used to run the family meatpacking business. Edward is eighty-four and George is eighty-two. Both are bachelors and have lived in this house all their lives.

In a study lined with pictures of their ancestors, Edward and George sketched a time-lapse picture of Weehawken and surroundings. The midtown skyline opposite had only one notable skyscraper, the Paramount Building on Forty-third Street, when they were young boys. By the time they were teenagers, the Chrysler Building, the Empire State, and Rockefeller Center had all gone up, and Midtown looked a lot like it does now. The Lincoln Tunnel came in in 1937; Edward, a boy of sixteen, was among the first to walk through it at the opening ceremony. Heading west from the tunnel, you could not go anyplace very directly, because that way was the swamp, which people called just "the swamp" and not the Meadowlands. Edward remembers looking across the swamp while on a family outing and predicting that one day a road would go straight across it. His words were prophetic; when he was just out of law school, construction started on Route 3. The road was finished across the Hackensack and Passaic rivers by 1950, and by '51 it was a busy highway with traffic jams.

Traffic had always been bad around here, Edward Fleckenstein pointed out. "Before the tunnel, there were long lines of wagons and cars, clear up to the top of the cliff, waiting to get on the ferry to the city," he said. "The tunnel was supposed to take care of that. In those days, we had an ambitious mayor, J. G. Meister, and he was a big booster for the tunnel. He said it would be such an honor for the town. One of the original ideas for the tunnel was for it to emerge on the other side of the next ridge, in Secaucus. And that probably would have been better, in hindsight, because of course it's more open over there and you wouldn't have the congestion of being confined in these hills. But Mayor Meister and other Weehawken supporters prevailed, and the tunnel came out in Weehawken. They said they would name it the Weehawken Midtown Tunnel, but, once there was the George Washington Bridge, naturally this had to be the Lincoln Tunnel."

Conversation soon turned to the town's other great event, the Burr–Hamilton duel. Referring to photocopies of historical documents, Edward Fleckenstein said where he thought the dueling grounds were and why he thought so. His brother excused himself to go to church services. Edward said he would show me where the site was, and he put on his fedora and topcoat and we got in my car. First, we stopped at the Hamilton memorial, a bust on a column at the cliff's edge. Whether Hamilton fired at Burr or deliberately into the air is unclear; he missed, in any event, and Burr's shot hit him in the abdomen. Hamilton knew at once that the wound was mortal. He fell against a large rock; the rock is now next to the column, part of the memorial. Hamilton was rowed back across the river to a friend's house in Greenwich Village, where he said good-bye to his wife and children and died the next day.

The site of the dueling grounds—about a hundred feet south of the end of the cliff, by Mr. Fleckenstein's estimation—takes some effort to visualize. In the car, he directed me to a street under the elevated highway and then onto a cinder lane near the waterfront. This place used to be a bay, he said. A cliff, roughly parallel to the present cliff but not as high, enclosed the bay at one end. There was a gravel beach accessible only by water, and above the beach, at the base of the cliff, a ledge about fifty feet long. Duelers used to row over from the city, pull their boats up on the beach, and fight their duels on the ledge. Construction of a country road leveled the cliff and ledge in 1859, and afterward railroad builders put tracks through. The landfill that buried the bay disguised the spot further.

Mr. Fleckenstein did not want to walk around in the eleven-degree cold and the wind, so after I took him home and thanked him, I came back. At least seventy duels were fought on this spot, he had told me. The combatants came here because laws against dueling weren't as strictly enforced in New Jersey. Hamilton and Burr were not the only famous duelers. DeWitt Clinton, governor of New York and father of the Erie Canal, fought a John Swartwout here and wounded him in the left leg about five inches above the ankle on the fifth shot. Commodore Oliver Hazard Perry, the hero of the Battle of Lake Erie ("We have met the enemy, and they are ours"), dueled Captain John Heath, neither man injured; Perry's second in that duel was Commodore Stephen Decatur ("Our country, right or wrong"), who was himself later killed in a duel in Maryland. Before Burr dueled Hamilton, he fought John Barker Church, Hamilton's brother-in-law, on this ground, neither man injured; and a Burr supporter fought and killed Hamilton's nineteen-year-old son, Philip (not here, but in nearby Paulus Hook), three years before the Burr-Hamilton duel. In all, at least thirty-six men died on the Weehawken dueling grounds.

Now the place is a construction side lot for the Lincoln Tunnel. There's an office trailer, a heap of pipe lengths, a portable john, some road-building stone, a chain-link fence, weeds, little orange plastic flags warning of buried cable. The long-ago life-and-death dramas I'd been picturing could not fit here; enterprise and time had painted out the past.

Then I looked across the river. You would have sat in the boat with your second, your pistols in their case on his lap, while someone rowed. For the twenty minutes or half an hour the journey took, you would have wondered, or tried not to wonder, about the condition in which you might come back. The far shore would grow closer, New York would diminish behind. The great city, the river in between, and this shore of scary possibility haven't changed. For questions of honor that we would find trivial or hard to understand, the touchy white men who founded our country sometimes shot each other to death within a thousand feet or so of where the Lincoln Tunnel toll booths are now.

(2004)

OUT OF OHIO

Recently I saw in a newspaper from Hudson, Ohio, my hometown, that they were about to tear down the town's water tower. In principle, I don't care anymore how things I used to love about Hudson change or disappear. Each time a big change happens, though, I feel a moment of resistance before my lack of caring returns. The town's water tower, built in the early 1900's, was its civic reference point, as its several white church steeples were its spiritual ones. The water tower was higher than they, and whenever you were walking in the fields—the town was surrounded by fields— you could scan the horizon for the water tower just above the tree line and know where you were. The cone-shaped top, and the cylindrical tank below it, gave the water tower the aspect of an old-time spaceship, though more squat. Its dull silver color and the prominent rivets in its sheet-metal side added to the antique Buck Rogers look. Or, to switch movies, the tower looked like the Tin Man in *The Wizard of Oz*. Two generations ago, water towers like this one could be found superintending small towns all over the Midwest and West. I'm sure the Tin Man was even based on them.

I lived in Hudson from when I was six until I was eighteen. Sometimes I try, usually without success, to describe how sweet it was to grow up in a small Ohio town forty years ago. As I get into the details, corniness tinges my voice, and a proprietary sentimentality that puts people off. I say the names of my friends from back then—Kent, Jimmy (called Dog), Susie, Bitsy, Kathy, Charlie (called Dunkie), Timmy, Paul—and they sound somehow wrong. They're like the names of characters in nostalgic mid-American movies or Bruce Springsteen songs, and I start to think of us as that myself, and a blurring sameness sets in, and the whole business defeats me. But then a friend from Hudson calls, or I run into somebody from there, or I hear the rattle of shopping-cart wheels in a supermarket parking lot, and for a second I remember how growing up in Hudson could be completely, even unfairly, sweet.

Most modern people don't belong anyplace as intimately as we belonged to Hudson. Now the town has grown and merged with northern Ohio exurbia, so it's hardly recognizable for what it was. Some of the old sense of belonging, though, remains. A while ago, I went back for a funeral. I took the bus from New York City to Cleveland overnight and then drove down to Hudson in the morning with my brother. We walked into Christ Church, our old church, now unfamiliar because of remodeling, and sat in the back. I saw not many people I knew. Then, over my shoulder, in the aisle, I heard a woman say, "I think I'll just sit here next to Sandy Frazier."

To return home, to have a person call me by name; and

to look up and remember her, forty-some years ago, as a junior-high girl in Bermuda shorts at the town's Ice Cream Social, an event sponsored by the League of Women Voters on the town green, where I and my friends chased her and her friends between tables and chairs and across the lawn flicking wadded-up pieces of paper cups at them with long-handled plastic ice-cream spoons, bouncing the missiles satisfyingly off the girls as they laughed and dodged—

I should finish that thought, and that sentence. But the service had begun for Cynthia, a friend to my family and me. She was dead at sixty-seven of Lou Gehrig's disease. Back in the 1960s, someone climbed the water tower and wrote Cynthia's name on it, billboard-large, a declaration of love. It stayed there above the trees for a long time, until the town painted it over. When I was eight or nine, Cynthia made a point of coming up and saying hello to me in the basement of the Congregational church. I was there, I think, because my mother was helping with the scenery for a play. When I was just out of high school, Cynthia heard me telling my friends a story in her living room, and afterward she told me I would be a writer. When I was in my twenties, I came back to town one night from hitchhiking someplace east or west, and I found nobody home at our house, so I went over to Cynthia's, and she put on a bathrobe and came downstairs and heated up a bowl of soup for me and sat with me at the island in the middle of her kitchen as I ate.

In those days I was constantly leaving town. Hudson was made for leaving. The Ohio Turnpike, also called Interstate 80, crossed the town from east to west behind a chain-link fence. The distant sound of traffic on the turnpike was part of the aural background of the town, like the rising and falling of the whistle in the Town Hall every noon. After the turnpike, other interstates came nearby. In Hudson Township, you could go from shady gravel road, to two-lane county asphalt, to far-horizon four-lane interstate highway in just a few turns of the steering wheel.

When I left the first time to go to college—the original leaving, which set a pattern for later ones—my plane to Boston was on a Sunday morning, and I spent all the preceding day and night going around town, seeing friends, saying good-bye, standing and talking under streetlights in hushed, excited tones. Early Sunday, I was lying on the floor of a living room with Kent, Bitsy, and Kathy, listening over and over to the song "Leaving on a Jet Plane." Nobody was saying anything. The girls were quietly crying, not so much about my leaving as about the overwhelmingness of everything: the year was 1969. I cried, and also pretended to cry, myself. From ground level I looked at the nap of the rug and the unswept-up miscellany under the couch. I would never be even a tenth as at home anywhere again.

Four years later, I graduated with a degree in General Studies and no clear plans. Mostly I wanted to go back home. I had had enough of the East, a place I was unable to make much sense of. My girlfriend at college, Sarah, whom I was too self-absorbed to appreciate, became fed up with my increasingly wistful hometown reminiscences as graduation day approached. "Don't invite me to your Ohio wedding" was one of her last remarks to me. After I received my diploma, my father came over to me in the courtyard of my dorm as I was talking to friends and hugged me so hard he lifted me off the ground. We loaded the trunk of the family Maverick with my belongings, the textbooks dumped in any which way, and drove straight home on Interstate 90 and the turnpike, arriving before dawn. I stayed awake and had some scrambled eggs my mother made, and then I went into the yard and watched the sunrise through the newly leafed trees. It rains a lot in northeastern Ohio, so the trees are extremely green. All around me, the summer landscape draped like a big hammock. I felt geographically well situated and defiantly at home.

I didn't bother to take my books out of the trunk of the car—just left them in there, rattling—and a few days later someone ran into my mother from behind on Middleton Road, and they scattered everywhere and got run over. My mother, as of course she would, carefully retrieved them. I still have several of them—for example, *The Power Elite* by C. Wright Mills, with a black Ohio tire tread running across the cover.

Why did Hudson enchant me? Why was life, there and then, so sweet? I think a million reasons happened to come together, none of which we grasped at the time. We had plenty of leisure. We had cars to drive. Gasoline was still so cheap it was practically free. Our parents, to whom the cars we drove belonged, had leisure, too. In their ease, they were inclined to take long vacations and indulge us kids. Fathers (and a few mothers) had steady jobs, pensions, health insurance. The economic difficulties that would later take a lot of those away and that I still don't understand had not yet visibly begun. Vietnam was winding down. The draft had just ended, removing a load from all our minds. Et cetera.

In my case, life was good, by comparison, because it had recently been so bad. The previous December, my fifteen-year-old brother, Fritz, had died of leukemia. After that, the last thing my parents wanted to do was to keep my other siblings and me from having any fun we could have. Dad and Mom would be gone a lot of that summer, traveling in India. At our house, I would be in charge.

And then, as a further reason for life's sweetness, there was hot, drowsy, hilly, expansive Ohio itself. Not so many people lived in Ohio then, and its commercial sprawl had narrower limits. Some of the local roads still were dirt and bisected working farms. Everybody still knew everybody. At Kepner's Bar on Main Street, I might run into a woman in a wild dress and hoop earrings who, it turned out, I'd known since first grade. To the west of town, on the turnpike, the highway went through a cut topped with a scenic (though otherwise unnecessary) bridge supported by a graceful arch that framed a megascreen view of the Cuyahoga River valley and sunlit points beyond. Too big to punish, we could now go where we wanted; a kid I knew got the urge to hitchhike to the East Coast one afternoon and set out in his bare feet, and traveled barefoot the whole journey. I was done with school—finally and thoroughly done. Vague possibilities shimmered in every direction.

Back then it seemed there was a lot more room, especially outdoors. In a town like Hudson every piece of ground did not have to account for itself, in real-estate terms, as it does today. On the edges of town and sometimes beside roads and buildings were plots of weedy, dusty, driven-over earth that no one had given much thought to since Hudson began. At the Academy, where I went to high school, the shadows of trees at sunset stretched three hundred yards across the school's lawns. Often on summer evenings we played Wiffle ball there. The game was like baseball, only with a plastic ball that didn't go as fast and wobbled in flight, and could be caught bare-handed. You didn't need shoes, either, in the lawn's soft grass.

After a game of Wiffle ball at sunset—after running enormously far across the lawn to catch foul balls, sliding shirtless into base on close plays, reclining itchily in the grass waiting to bat, quitting the game only when it was too dark to see the ball—we would go to the beverage store downtown and stand in the pleasantly frigid walk-in cooler, deciding whether to buy the evening's supply of Stroh's beer by the twelve-pack or the case. And then the evening would continue. At this hour, girls we knew might be sitting on somebody's front porch smoking cigarettes. Twenty minutes of driving around would discover them.

That summer, a woman I'd gone out with when she was a girl happened to be in town. Her family had moved to Wheaton, Illinois, but she had come back to stay with her sister, who lived in an apartment above a store on Main Street. I climbed the outdoor stairs and knocked on the apartment door, and Susie came out, keeping one ear open for her sleeping nephew, whom she was babysitting. We were kissing at the bottom of the stairs in the shadows when she considered me for a moment and declared, "You're a real person."

The "you" was emphasized: "*You're* a real person." She meant this not as a compliment but as a statement of fact. I understood what she meant. After growing up in Hudson, where anybody you met you already knew, you found it hard to take people from anyplace else quite seriously. They might be nice, and interesting, and all, but they had a transitory quality. Only people from Hudson you'd known forever could be completely real.

Now I see Hudson as the place where I was spun and spun throughout my childhood in order to have maximum velocity when it finally let me go. My leaving-for-good happened like this:

I hung around that summer until my presence became otiose. Friends' parents started asking me how long I would be in town. My parents, back from India, began to suggest chores, like mowing the lawn. There's a certain nightmare time-warp feeling that can come over you—a sense that you're your present size but sitting in your old desk from elementary school, with your knees sticking up on the sides. The feeling can motivate you to plunge into any uncertainty, just so long as it's present tense. One morning in late August, I packed a suitcase, jumped the turnpike fence, and began to hitchhike west.

First, I went to visit my best friend and former neighbor, Don, in Colchester, Illinois. Colchester is smaller than Hudson and more intoxicatingly Midwestern. The backyards on

Don's street were all clotheslines and garden rows of corn, and beyond the corn ran the tracks of a main rail line bound for St. Louis. Don and his friends and I used to smoke dope and sit by the tracks at night waiting for the eleven o'clock train. At first, it was a little, faraway light, and then suddenly it grew into a blaring blue-white beam and gigantic noise pounding immediately by. Then in a while the night would be its quiet self again. Just to lie in the back bedroom of Don's house with the curtains billowing inward on the breeze was middle-of-the-country nirvana for me.

From Colchester I continued on to Chicago, where I got a job on a European-style skin magazine published by *Playboy*. The magazine's editor had written to the *Harvard Lampoon*, which I had worked for in college, and had offered a job to any *Lampoon* person who wanted one. The offices were cavelike, with halls resembling tunnels and fragrant dark brown corkboard paneling on the walls. In a short while, I learned that writing captions for photos of naked women is a particular talent, one that is surprisingly difficult to fake. I quit the day I was supposed to get a company ID card, which I feared would be a raised bunny head—the *Playboy* logo—stamped on a photo of my face.

Then I lay around my small North Side apartment for a few months on the bare mattress that was its only furniture and read books or looked at the plaster floret on the ceiling. Somewhere I had come across Hemingway's list of the novels he thought it essential for every writer to know and I started in on them. I also spent weeks at a time in uninterrupted, not uncomfortable despair. On Wednesdays, I would go to the newsstand across from the Ambassador East Hotel and buy the latest issue of *The New Yorker,* and then on my mattress I would read every word in it, including the columns of small type in the front. When Pauline Kael reviewed a movie by Sam Peckinpah, I told Susie that Kael had called him "a great and savage artist," and that I wanted people someday to say the same about me. Susie was going to school at the University of Northern Iowa at Cedar Falls. I sometimes took long Greyhound bus rides out to visit her.

My grandmother, a can-do person who enjoyed the challenge of setting wayward relatives on their feet, sent me many letters telling me to come visit her in Florida, and after about the fourth letter I agreed. Before I left Chicago, I gave up my apartment. The landlord was glad to get rid of me. He said that he thought my mattress, surrounded as it was by all the books and magazines I'd been reading, constituted a fire hazard. From Chicago I rode Greyhound buses for forty-five hours to Key West. On one bus I saw a skinny white guy with combed-high hair try to pick up a black woman sitting next to him, and when she politely moved to another seat he drank a pint or two of whiskey, began to shout at his reflection in the bus window, asked the old woman in front of him if she was wearing a wig, pulled her hair to find out, and eventually left the bus in handcuffs under the escort of the highway patrol, an expression of calm inevitability on his face. Between Georgia and Miami, I listened through the night to a Vietnam veteran with hair longer than Joni Mitchell's talk about a Vietnamese woman he had killed during the war, and about many other topics, his words flowing unstoppably and pathologically until I came almost to hate him. When I finally shot him an angry look, he gave me back a stare of such woefulness and misery that I was ashamed. Out of South Miami I sat next to a psychiatrist who explained to me in psychological terms why the passengers sitting near him objected to his chainsmoking. He was the only seatmate I openly argued with. When my grandmother met me at the Key West bus station, I was furious at her for all I'd been through.

Unlike my parents, Grandmother did not believe in depression. If my mother fell into a gloom, she usually nurtured it into a dark and stationary front that hung over the kitchen for days. As for my father, his strategy when he became depressed was to move from a regular level of depression as much farther down the scale as he could possibly go, getting more and more depressed and thinking up consequent sorrows and disasters of every kind until he reached a near-panic state. Then when he came to himself again, and looked at the actual situation, it seemed not so terrible after all. Grandmother's approach, by contrast, was never to give depression the smallest advantage. Whenever she sensed its approach, she attacked it and routed it and slammed the door.

In Key West, she didn't even allow me to be horizontal for longer than eight hours of sleeping a night. Early in the mornings, she appeared at the front desk of the Southern Cross Hotel, where she had rented me a small room, and she sent the plump and sarcastic German manager to pound on my door with a German-accented witticism. Then she would give me breakfast and hurry me off to the job she had found for me, doing gardening work for a lady even older than she, Minona Seagrove. Minona Seagrove walked very slowly and couldn't really bend down, but she loved to garden, and every day I served as her robot gardening arms, trimming palmetto fronds and planting bulbs while she stood behind me and said what to do. In the evenings, Grandmother made dinner for me and my cousin Libby, who was also visiting. Then sometimes we would play long games of Scrabble with Grandmother, her friend Marjorie Houck, and a very old English lady named Mavis Strange, who consistently won, using words that are in the dictionary but nobody has heard of.

Grandmother's closest friend, Betty Stock, had a daughter named Isabel who worked for *The New Yorker*. Under the name Andy Logan, Isabel wrote the Around City Hall column for the magazine. Just before graduation, I had halfheartedly applied to *The New Yorker* for a staff writing job. Grandmother said if I tried again she would ask Betty to ask Isabel to put in a word with the editor for me. This idea seemed kind of far-fetched, but I said okay: I hadn't brooked Grandmother in anything so far. Grandmother didn't like my hair, so she sent me to her longtime hairdresser and had him cut it. It came out looking bad, though not as bad as I had expected. Grandmother also went through my wardrobe, if it could be called a wardrobe, and singled out a pair of khaki slacks, a shirt, and a blue sweater as acceptable clothing to wear for New York job interviews. I trusted her unquestioningly as an authority on what well-dressed office workers in New York City wore.

After a month or so of this retooling, Grandmother was satisfied and ready for me to move on. Libby drove me in Grandmother's Ford Fairlane a few miles up the Keys to a good place to hitchhike. In a night-and-day hitchhiking marathon, I made it from the Keys to Morgantown, Kentucky, where my friend Kent was doing volunteer work for the Glenmary Home Missioners. Along the way, I got some wacky Southern rides, including one across South Carolina with a Post Office driver in a small refrigerated truck carrying, he said, "human eyeballs." He was taking them to an eye bank somewhere.

In late afternoon, I arrived at the slant-floored mountain shack Kent had rented, and I was so tired that I immediately lay down and fell asleep on a bed in a side room. It happened that Kent was having a party for the entire community that night. As the guests came in, they piled their coats on top of the bed, on top of me. At the party's height a man and a woman entered the room and closed the door and, not knowing I was there, lay down on the coats and began to talk about the extramarital affair they were having. I emerged from sleep to the sound of their French-movie-type dialogue: "Oh, Roger, I've felt like crying for the last three days!" "Oh, Arliss, [mumble mumble mumble]." Then suddenly the door opened, and from it, like a superloud PA system, the voice of the outraged husband: "Get out of that fuckin' bed, Roger!" The two men adjourned outside for a fistfight while the woman stayed on the coats, sobbing. I began to stir, poking part of my head out from under. The sobbing stopped; silence; then, in complete bafflement, "Who's *he?*"

A few days later, I was back in Hudson. At this slow time of year, none of my friends were around, except Kathy. She had a job at a small, classy store on Main Street that sold women's clothes. I thought that now would be a good opportunity to tell her of the crush I had on her, but as I stood in the store watching her refold sweaters or sat with her on the couch in her family's TV room talking about what our other friends were doing, the moment never came up. Late one night, I went over to her house with an idea of throwing some pebbles at her window, waking her and telling her how I felt. When I approached through the backyards, the light was still on in her bedroom; as I got closer I saw in the dimness a guy at the edge of her lawn staring so raptly at her window that he never noticed me.

I faded back into the next yard and cut across it and then went to the sidewalk, and as I passed by the front of Kathy's house I saw a cigarette glow on the front steps. She was sitting there and didn't seem at all surprised to see me. I told her about the guy in her backyard and she smiled. She had a quick smile that went horizontally, like a rubber band stretched between two fingers. The corners of it were so cute they drew your eyes into close-up frame. With undisguisable happiness she said, "That was John."

And so on to New York City. Early one morning before work, Kathy gave me a ride to Exit 13 on the turnpike, just east of town. Local hitchhiking wisdom said that more eastbound trucks got on the highway there. After a friendly hug across the front seat I got out and she drove away. I carried my same suitcase and a cardboard sign on which I'd written "NYC" in large letters with a Magic Marker. I was keyed up. I hadn't asked my parents for money—some of my Minona Seagrove earnings still remained—and I intended not to come back without something to show. I stood, heroic to myself, on the shoulder of the on-ramp in the smell of diesel and the gusts from traffic blowing by. After half an hour or so, a truck pulled over. That moment is always a thrill, when the air brakes hiss and the big machine swerves over and stops just for you. I ran to it, threw my suitcase up through the open door, and climbed the rungs to the cab.

I didn't go very far that day. Many short rides and long waits put me after nightfall at a truck stop in central Pennsylvania. The place had a dormitory floor upstairs and a dozen beds for truckers, and bathrooms with showers. I signed the register in my own name, boldly wrote down that I drove for Carolina Freight, and paid my five dollars for a narrow metal-frame bed. I slept well in a room with a changing group of truckers, each of whom put in his few sleeping hours determinedly and then was gone. In the morning I showered, ate a big breakfast in the restaurant, and, caffeinated and pleased with the day so far, stood by the parking-lot exit with my sign.

The truck that pulled over for me there looked so unpromising that I hesitated before getting in. The tractor was gas-powered, not diesel, with a rusty white cab and a small trailer—the kind of rig, smaller than an eighteen-wheeler, that hauls carnival rides. Its driver appeared equally off-brand. He had strands of black hair around his too-white face and he lacked a few teeth. After saying hello, he told me that he had just taken a lot of methamphetamines. I asked if he was feeling them yet, and he whipped off his sunglasses and said, "Look at my eyes!" Bedspring spirals of energy seemed to be radiating from his black irises. He was beating on the steering wheel with his palms, fiddling with the all-static radio, and moving from one conversational topic to another randomly.

It is perhaps unfair to say that drivers of carnival trucks are horny guys; free-floating lust howls down every highway in the world, sweeping all kinds of people along. This particular speed-popping driver, however, closely fit the horny-guy profile. As his conversation caromed around, it kept returning to, and finally settled on, the subject of a whorehouse he said was not far up the road. He talked about how much he liked it, and what he did there, and the girls who worked in it, and the old man who owned it, and how popular he, the driver, was there.

Soon the driver was going to suggest that he and I make a visit to this whorehouse. I could tell; clearly his drift tended no other way. As he went on, I considered how I would respond. Sanity said, obviously, no. Under no circumstances go to a whorehouse with this guy. Say thanks but no thanks, and jump out as soon as possible. I was ready to be sane and do that. But then I thought . . . I wasn't bound for New York just to demur and make my apologies. Begging off of anything at this point didn't feel right. New York City was the big time, and I wanted to be big-time when I got there. When the moment came to jump, I intended to jump. Right then the guy turned to me with a wicked and challenging glint to his sunglasses. Almost before the words left his mouth I thanked him politely and said that yes, going to this whorehouse sounded like an excellent idea.

For a while after that, the guy fell silent. I flattered myself that maybe I'd taken him by surprise. He turned the truck off the highway and proceeded along a two-lane country road. I had no idea what I would do when we got to the whorehouse. The thought of going to it scared me dizzy. I figured I would come up with a plan when I had to. Ahead I saw a tall, narrow three-story house, its bare windows sealed inside with blinds. A small neon beer sign lit a side door. "There she is!" the driver said, perking up. No cars were in the gravel parking lot as he coasted in, downshifting. He leaned across the dash and pulled over by the side door to examine it closely, giving a few light taps on the horn. No reply or sign of life. More taps on the horn. A few minutes passed. Then, reluctantly, he concluded that no one was about, and he headed back to the highway.

Oh, the intense and private joy of the uncalled bluff! Until now I had experienced it only in games. This felt a hundred times greater than any game. Keeping my face nonchalant, I exulted inwardly and made a resolve that in my new life in New York City I would bluff whenever the occasion arose. At that moment on the road in the middle of Pennsylvania, I quit living in Hudson and began to live in the world.

The guy let me off someplace in eastern Pennsylvania. By then, the pills he had taken had evidently set him back down, and he looked different, kind of shriveled and mumbly, behind the wheel. I was relieved to be shut of him and out of his spooky cab, and I shouted with the pleasure of being alone as soon as his truck was out of sight. The next ride I got was with a guy about my age from San Isidro,

Costa Rica. He must've been part Indian, because he had straight black hair like a Sioux's and an Aztec nose. He was littler than a Sioux, though, and olive skinned. He drove a big-engine car, the kind they had back then that looked like slabs, and its rear seat was full of cardboard boxes of his stuff. He had lived in Chicago and was moving to New York City, he said. I told him I was, too. With a companion we knew better each of us might have been cooler and more re-strained, but as he maneuvered the big car through Jersey traffic we cheered at the first glimpse of the city skyline faintly gray on the horizon.

I hadn't seen a lot of cities then, and I didn't know that New York, to a traveler coming from the west, affords the best first-time, big-city view in the U.S.A. The guy from Costa Rica and I cruised across the long and splendid drum-roll of open-sky swamp up to the Hudson River. Then we swerved down the elevated highway toward the Lincoln Tunnel, and the city suddenly and manifestly filled the windshield and side windows, rising from the Hudson as if lifted by eyelids when you opened your eyes. No skyline I know of is its equal; across the windows it ran, left to right, like a long and precise and detailed and emphatic sentence ending with the double exclamation points of the World Trade Center towers.

It was a mild day in early March, just before rush hour. Lights had come on in some of the buildings, and dusk was beginning to gather in the spaces between them. We went through the Lincoln Tunnel and popped up on the city floor, with buildings and vehicles impending all around. Our windows were open; the city smelled like coffee, bus exhaust, and fingernail polish. The Costa Rican was going to stay with relatives in Queens, a place as exotic to me then as Costa Rica. I was going to Greenwich Village to meet my friend David, who had told me he could find me a place to stay. I got out at Thirty-fourth and Seventh, the southwest corner. When I pass by that corner occasionally today, I still think of it as the place where I landed. The Costa Rican and I wished each other good luck, without pretending to exchange phone numbers (we didn't have them, anyway) or saying we'd keep in touch. We were now each a little part of the other's past, and in New York the past was gone.

(2005)